Parents' Education as Autism Therapists

of related interest

Asperger's Syndrome
A Guide for Parents and Professionals
Tony Attwood
ISBN 1 85302 577 1

Pretending to be Normal
Living with Asperger's Syndrome
Liane Holliday Willey
ISBN 1 85302 749 9

Eating an Artichoke
A Mother's Perspective on Asperger's Syndrome
Echo Fling
ISBN 1 85302 711 1

Finding Out about Asperger's Syndrome, High Functioning Autism and PDD
Gunilla Gerland
ISBN 1 85302 840 1

Small Steps Forward
Games and Activities for Pre-School Children with Special Needs
Sarah Newman
ISBN 1 85302 643 3

A Positive Approach to Autism
Stella Waterhouse
ISBN 1 85302 808 8

Autism and Play
Jannik Beyer and Lone Gammeltoft
ISBN 1 85302 845 2

Autism: An Inside–Out Approach
An Innovative Look at the Mechanics of 'Autism'
and its Developmental 'Cousins'
Donna Williams
ISBN 1 85302 387 6

Autism and Sensing
The Unlost Instinct
Donna Williams
ISBN 1 85302 612 3

Through the Eyes of Aliens
A Book about Autistic People
Jasmine Lee O'Neill
ISBN 1 85302 710 3

Children with Autism, 2nd Edition
Diagnosis and Intervention to Meet Their Needs
Colwyn Trevarthen, Kenneth Aitken, Despina Papoudi and Jacqueline Robarts
ISBN 1 85302 555 0

Parents' Education as Autism Therapists

Applied Behaviour Analysis in Context

Edited by
Mickey Keenan, Ken P. Kerr
and Karola Dillenburger

Foreword by Bobby Newman

Jessica Kingsley Publishers
London and Philadelphia

First published in the United Kingdom in 2000 by
Jessica Kingsley Publishers Ltd,
116 Pentonville Road, London
N1 9JB, England
and
325 Chestnut Street,
Philadelphia PA 19106, USA.

www.jkp.com

© Copyright 2000 Jessica Kingsley Publishers

Second impression 2002

Library of Congress Cataloging in Publication Data
A CIP catalog record for this book is available from the Library of Congress

British Library Cataloguing in Publication Data
A CIP catalog record for this book is available from the British Library

ISBN 1 85302 778 2 pb

Printed and Bound in Great Britain by
Athenaeum Press, Gateshead, Tyne and Wear

Contents

Acknowledgements

We thank all those who have helped in practical terms or otherwise in the setting up of the PEAT group and in the completion of this book.

Mickey Keenan
Ken P. Kerr
Karola Dillenburger

Foreword

I don't own a sweatshirt or jacket from the university I attended. It's not that Queens College isn't a fine institution, but somehow I just never felt the burning need or desire to own one. The only college apparel that I own is from the University of Ulster at Coleraine in Northern Ireland. For me, the University of Ulster at Coleraine will forever be in my memory as standing for what a university ought to: the pursuit and application of knowledge for practical and philosophical benefit.

I first came to the University of Ulster for a week-long visit after receiving an invitation to visit Northern Ireland from Dr Michael Keenan ('Mickey'). Mickey and I knew each other from the internet and a brief meeting at a conference in Washington, DC. Mickey is a student and practitioner of the science known as Applied Behavior Analysis. He and I began speaking (actually, typing) to each other when he posted a message on an internet forum as a behavior analyst who was feeling a little isolated in his homeland, without other behavior analysts to collaborate with. I reassured him that even in the US, where most of the membership of the International Association for Behavior Analysis resides, behavior analysts tend to feel isolated. Applied Behavior Analysis (ABA) just isn't a very widely studied field.

Mickey first impressed me with his knowledge of the field and his desire to teach it to others. Always looking for new ways to teach and inspire his students, Mickey asked me if I had any interesting demonstrations for students. I sent him a reprint of an article I wrote with some colleagues and the protocols for a silly little experiment I do with my experimental psychology students where they study classical conditioning by tickling each other. Mickey showed me his computer expertise at this point, creating computer animation to demonstrate the experiment's procedure. Mickey's computerized programmed instruction is as good an introduction to Behavior Analysis as I've seen.

My own work centers around applying Behavior Analysis to the problems faced by those who are diagnosed with autism and related disorders. It was as a result of this work that my involvement with Mickey's work was once again revived. What must be understood is that when I began my career, Applied Behavior Analysis was not held in the highest regard. In fact, it was often dismissed as a rather simple-minded approach to human behavior. In the 1970s, there were even laws proposed in certain states of the US to bar ABA practises. If I may steal from Richard Foxx, one of the best behavior analysts going, the degree to which people denigrate Behavior Analysis is generally in inverse proportion to the extent that they understand it. In my opinion, Behavior Analysis has matured sufficiently that it should be considered its own discipline and no longer be considered a sub-field of psychology. The closest analogy I can make is that between chiropractors and osteopaths. They may look at some of the same phenomena, but their methods and commitment to scientific methods are so disparate that there is little room for discussion.

In 1987, a study was published describing the work of O. Ivar Lovaas and colleagues. In this landmark study, Behavior Analysis was intensively applied with pre-school-aged children diagnosed with autism. When the dust cleared at the end of the study, nearly one half of the intensively treated children were indistinguishable from other children their age. They had completely lost any vestige of their prior diagnosis.

What was most amazing was not the result of this study, but the way in which it was received. Most people tried to explain the findings away. If the kids improved, they weren't really autistic in the first place. Others objected that students weren't placed into experimental and control groups randomly, but rather based upon if there was a qualified person available to oversee treatment. It was a prototype of failing to see the forest for the trees, and most people did not take notice of ABA.

The outlook for ABA changed drastically in the early 1990s. A book was published entitled *Let Me Hear Your Voice*. The author, Catherine Maurice, was not a behavior analyst. She was not a scientist. She was a mommy. She was a mommy who described how her children emerged from autism through the use of ABA. The floodgates opened. Suddenly EVERYONE wanted ABA services. My answering machine, and that of anyone who was known for doing ABA with people with autism, was filled on a nightly basis with messages from people who had heard of the work and pulled our names from the phone book. I remember thinking that if there was another Bobby Newman in the phone book, he was probably cursing me to hell for all the phone calls he was getting with people looking for me.

This explosion of popularity has been a mixed blessing. On the one hand, many more people than ever are receiving quality behavioral interventions and are reaping the benefits. On the other hand, there are not nearly enough trained behavior analysts to meet the need. As nature abhors a vacuum, the untrained step in where there is a need and no trained people are available.

In almost every corner of the globe, Behavior Analysis is not a controled field in the sense that there are no licensing exams and/or state recognized credentials. That process is only slowly coming into being now. In the meanwhile, those who are seeking ABA services have to rely on rather dubious word of mouth to ascertain the quality of those they seek to hire. Many 'behavior analysts' have no degrees. At best, they worked as assistants under a behavior analyst. In this field, unfortunately, what you don't know can hurt your client a whole lot.

It was this explosion of interest in ABA that brought me to Northern Ireland, and the first series of trainings I did at the University of Ulster. The parents and professionals, authors of the text you now explore, asked me if I would come over to provide a series of introductory trainings regarding the wonderful field known as ABA. Honored, I accepted.

There were some idiomatic issues to work out. I would describe a technique for a parent to try out at home. They would return the next day and say 'It worked a treat!' I would pause and say, 'Is that good?' One parent described her child's behavior and finished by saying 'At the end of the day, he's not talking'. Not knowing that 'at the end of the day' means to sum up, I replied 'Well, does he talk in the morning?' The silence was deafening.

ABA is riding the wave of popularity now, and the only thing that can kill it is the proliferation of people who claim to be behavior analysts who really don't know how to do it. Every time an untrained person fails, calling what they do Behavior Analysis, confidence in the field is undermined. We must train more people properly, educate people as to what ABA really is and really isn't, and seek to give credentials to those who are properly qualified. This book represents the efforts of people who are trying to do just that, and I'm proud to have been a part of it.

One of my first instructors, Claire Poulson, once warned that Behavior Analysis would never be the most popular treatment. It didn't offer miracle cures, but rather steady and sometimes grueling work over a period of years. This statement captured the state of affairs before *Let Me Hear Your Voice*. In certain quarters, now, behavior analysts are the most popular kids on the street. This reputation is deserved. I invite you to come and learn why.

Bobby Newman PhD, CBA
Association in Manhattan for Autistic Children

Preface

On 17 March 1997 an article appeared in a local newspaper in Northern Ireland (*The Belfast Telegraph*) about Colin (not his real name) who had been diagnosed with Asperger's Syndrome. The article outlined the successes that had been achieved with the child after his General Practitioner had referred him to Dr Mickey Keenan, a behaviour analyst at the University of Ulster. Such was the public interest in this article that a public meeting was called to inform parents about the behavioural methods used for teaching children with autism. In June 1997, at the invitation of Dr Keenan, Professor Newman from the Association in Manhattan for Autistic Children spent one week hosting workshops on Behaviour Analysis for parents and professionals interested in autism. As a result of this workshop parents formed a group called Parents' Education as Autism Therapists (PEAT) which subsequently gained charitable status. Outside of this group and the voluntary work of Dr Keenan along with consultation by Dr Kerr (Director of Training for PEAT) there is no statutory organisation that caters for the education of these parents in the methods of Behaviour Analysis. Indeed, throughout the whole of Ireland there are no behaviour analysts trained in the methods used in early intervention with these children. The idea for this book stemmed from the need to alter this state of affairs. PEAT parents and behaviour analysts set out together to offer a text that would contribute to the effective education of other parents and their children diagnosed with autism.

The book has six chapters. In Chapter 1 Hillary Johnston, Barbara Hanna, Laura McKay and Mary O'Cahan give a parent's perspective of what Applied Behaviour Analysis (ABA) means for them and their children. They discuss the relevant principles involved in setting up behaviour analytic programmes and describe some of the procedures that are most often used for children with autism.

In Chapter 2, Ken P. Kerr puts the parents' perspective into the academic context. Behaviour Analysis has been applied with children who are diagnosed with autism for a very long time and its effectiveness has been well documented in the academic literature. This chapter describes the key findings, identifies the criteria for effective behaviour analytic intervention, outlines the importance of parent/family input, and corrects some of the inaccuracies that have crept into public perception. Scientific evidence strongly indicates that Applied Behaviour Analysis is indeed the therapy of choice for children with autism.

In Chapter 3 Ian Taylor introduces the important area of functional assessment and functional analysis and relates this to the kind of challenging behaviour all too often seen in children with autism. He demonstrates how such techniques can be used to develop effective interventions suited to the needs of the child.

Chapter 4 describes the first year of treatment for Colin. Laura McKay (Colin's mother), Mickey Keenan, and Karola Dillenburger outline many of the procedures used during the year of Colin's treatment. Data collected by Colin's mother are presented in the sequence in which the work was carried out to illustrate the precision and amount of work necessary to apply Behaviour Analysis properly. Pertinent issues that arise are also discussed.

In Chapter 5 Ken P. Kerr replies to the question 'What do we want to teach our children?' by looking at an ABA curriculum and identifying some of the main tasks that are commonly taught. He illustrates the sophistication of ABA procedures developed by PEAT parents.

In Chapter 6 Mickey Keenan, Ken P. Kerr, and Karola Dillenburger conclude the book by pointing out that, although there is ample evidence for the effectiveness of behaviour analysis and parents' education as autism therapists, these findings have not permeated all professional circles. They emphasise the child's right to scientifically validated and effective treatment and point to some problems that parents may encounter should they decide to pursue training in the science of behaviour.

CHAPTER 1

Applied Behaviour Analysis
A Parents' Perspective

Hillary Johnston, Barbara Hanna,
Laura McKay and Mary O'Cahan

Successful child rearing is an essential skill for any parent. For most of us this skill is handed down from our own parents and society in general. In real terms this means that rather than relying on any formal instruction to help us, we bring up our children using skills based largely upon common sense and a willingness to do our best. These methods are, by-and-large, successful in everyday situations. However, when it comes to more difficult aspects of developing skills in our children, we need something more dependable than good will. Applied Behaviour Analysis, the systematic implementation of scientifically proven behavioural principles offers just that. Aimed at enhancing people's lives in ways that they or their carers feel are important, it includes a variety of methods and techniques which can be used to promote, decrease, or maintain skills for daily living. In this chapter we will outline the basics of Applied Behaviour Analysis. We discuss the relevant principles involved in setting up programmes to develop desirable behaviour and we describe some of the procedures most often used for children with autism.

Over the past year and a half we have been part of a group of parents who each wanted to become educated as therapists for their own child. We meet once a month with trained behaviour analysts, learn about Applied Behaviour Analysis, present the work that we have carried out during the month with our child, and discuss and plan how we should proceed over the next month. As parents of children with autism we have written this chapter to outline our understanding and use of Applied Behaviour Analysis. You will find that this chapter reflects the writing process as we pass the baton of authorship to one another. We have used examples of our work with our own children to illustrate the aspects of ABA that are discussed. Consequently, you will read about four different children throughout this chapter. (Some of us have changed our names and most of us have changed the name of our child.)

What is Applied Behaviour Analysis?

Applied Behaviour Analysis is the application of the science called Behaviour Analysis. The history of Behaviour Analysis reaches back into the early part of the twentieth century. Since then behaviour analytic scientists have set out to uncover the natural laws that are in operation when behaviour occurs. Applied Behaviour Analysis is therefore the application of the knowledge gained by these scientists with the aim of enhancing the life of individuals or groups of people.

The definitions found in the dictionary clarify what ABA means in reality for parents and their children with autism. There are many definitions of the word 'applied', the most appropriate one in this context being 'practice', although to those of us actively involved in Applied Behaviour Analysis the definition 'hard work' would seem more appropriate. 'Analysis' is a necessary part of 'wanting to understand', and usually it involves looking at the results of our work to see what sort of picture emerges from the information collected. As for 'behaviour', this can be described as anything people do. In most cases behaviour can be observed and recorded, for example skills such as playing and talking. However, some behaviours cannot be so easily observed. They happen inside the person, such as feelings or thoughts. Yet, these too are behaviours that can be analysed and, if need be, changed (more on this later).

How does Behaviour Analysis view autism?

Professionals diagnosed my child as having autism when he was about two years old. I was told then that no one really knows why a child develops autism, that it is a life-long condition, and that the best thing I could do for my child is to learn to cope with his condition and accept him as he is. In brief, I was told that he 'had' autism. That is, they used the term 'autism' to explain his condition. They advised me that I should accept that he had a characteristic and unique learning style and that I should learn to understand his autistic mind.

When I first learned about Behaviour Analysis I was also told that no one really knows why a child develops autism. However, I was then told that the term 'autism' did not explain anything. I was told that the term was really best viewed as a descriptive label, a catch-all phrase, that summed up how my child was likely to behave: sometimes he would do things too often (behavioural excesses) and sometimes he would do things too seldom (behavioural deficits). I began thinking of my child in these terms and soon found that there were certain aspects of his behaviour that I would like to see decreased, for example, stimming (self-stimulatory behaviours). There were other behaviours that I would like to see becoming stronger, more frequent and more consistent, for example, using speech. I was told that the best way to accept him was to help him redress this balance by teaching him to do certain things more often and others less often. In doing this we would help him to develop his full potential. In brief, I was told that a range of general principles of behaviour that had been discovered by Behaviour Analysts over the years could be harnessed to help my son, just as they could be applied to help any other human being.

What are the aims of Behaviour Analysis?

One of the main differences between traditional psychology and Applied Behaviour Analysis is that most traditional psychologists analyse human behaviour by using group averages. In so doing they can lose that sensitive touch that is necessary in the analysis of individual behaviour and in the arranging of individually tailored learning environments. In contrast, Applied Behaviour Analysis has developed procedures specifically geared to measuring individual differences in behaviour. This has lead to behaviour analysts becoming experts in tailoring individualised treatment programmes. The important word here is 'tailored'. As with any suit of clothes, those that fit best are those that are specifically designed for the person who will wear them.

Although every child is capable of learning, for some children an extra effort is necessary to maximise their learning. Behaviour Analysis supplies the framework for this 'extra effort' for those who care for these children. This framework shows how the individual learning environment of these children can be specifically tailored to their needs in a flexible way that evolves as progress is made.

When behaviour change is called for (i.e., therapy), the emphasis should be on bringing out the best in an individual. If you don't try to bring out the best in an individual you will never know what they can achieve and what their limitations are. This does not mean that Applied Behaviour Analysis is not accepting of the individual with autism. On the contrary, a crucial part of the process of designing a learning environment is acceptance of where the individual is at any time; that is, knowing what they can or can not do. However, this acceptance is not to be equated with reluctance to proceed further, to probe into what an individual can achieve if their learning environment is matched to their current level of skills.

Why do I use Applied Behaviour Analysis with my child?

As a parent, Applied Behaviour Analysis gives me the skills and knowledge to expand my son Jack's learning potential, to teach him new behaviours such as using his knife and fork appropriately, or to address certain problem behaviours, such as when he is screaming to get something he wants. Behaviour Analysis gives me a practical means to teach him as much as is possible and to manage and cope with problem behaviours. I now don't feel so isolated and overwhelmed with the everyday struggle of coping with Jack, and I feel more in control of situations that arise. In the past Jack was the one in control, which ultimately lead to him getting his own way in many situations. This was fine for the short term but did no one any good in the long term, and certainly did not solve the problem.

The main objectives of Applied Behaviour Analysis for me are to help Jack learn various new skills from simple responses that society takes for granted, such as looking at others (eye contact), to complex acts such as spontaneous communication and social interaction. The ability to analyse Jack's behaviour thoroughly enables me to teach Jack the difference between appropriate and inappropriate behaviour, while ensuring that the learning process is fun and interesting for both of us!

How do I use Behaviour Analysis?

Defining behaviour

Applied Behaviour Analysis has developed a wide range of ways for teaching specific skills. We will describe some of those most often used with children who have autism later in this chapter. The first thing I do before deciding how to arrange a new learning environment for Jack is to decide what it is I want him to learn. This is called identifying the 'target behaviour'. The target behaviour is the behaviour we want to see afterwards, after he has gone through the experiences that I will arrange for him. (By the way, scientists have their own language for talking about arranging a new learning environment. They talk about designing an 'intervention'.)

Of course it is very important to choose the right target behaviours. The target behaviour should always be something that will help your child lead a more fulfilled life. This will obviously differ from child to child and from family to family. Older children can sometimes be helped to decide what it is they want to learn, but for younger ones, parents may have to decide on their behalf what should be learned. Behaviour analysts can assist in the decision making process. For example, I decided to work with Jack on a problem behaviour that had been going on for some time. When Jack came home from school he had started to scream if there was no Cola waiting for him. This screaming could go on for half an hour to an hour. I was finding it increasingly hard to cope with this situation and he did not enjoy it either. When I decided to work on this behaviour with him, my first step was to define what I meant by screaming.

You might think that surely screaming is screaming. But on closer inspection you will find that there is much more going on than meets the eye. For example, I had to ask myself whether it was the intensity of the screaming that bothered me, or the number of times he screamed, or the time of day when he did it, or the duration of the screaming, or the fact that he screamed at all. Once I had defined screaming more precisely, I was be able to measure it and thus monitor the effectiveness of a new learning environment that was designed to replace it with more appropriate behaviour (see Chapter 5).

Measuring behaviour

After defining screaming, the target behaviour for our next piece of work, my next step was to keep an ABC chart of his screaming behaviour for approximately 10 days. Some of the most important aspects of Behaviour Analysis are involved here. We will describe what it means to keep an ABC chart in a moment. First, let us look at the fact that behaviour can be measured. It might come as a surprise that someone would want to measure behaviour. Why would you want to do it? How do you go about it? Do you use a ruler, or a piece of string, or a weighing machine? Can behaviour really be measured? Of course it can and in fact it is not only scientists who do it; we all do it, only scientists do it more precisely. For example, we know who in our family is most likely to do the dishes, who is most likely to make the tea, and who is most likely to cut the grass in the summer. You would be able to answer, if asked, which of your children gets up first in the morning and which one is more likely to need more sleep than the others. Each of these examples includes behaviours, or sequences of behaviours, that have a beginning and an end. Your ability to specify the behaviour that is happening at any moment is the first step in measuring it. After that it is a relatively straightforward step to quantifying it. When we say someone is likely to do something, we could say that they do it once a day, twice a day, or three times a week. It means that we have found a way to quantify behaviour along one particular dimension. To put it another way, we now can say how much of that behaviour occurs. That's measuring behaviour!

Behaviour analysts have developed a science that shows us how to measure behaviour precisely. In fact, there are quite a few ways in which this can be done. Once we have defined the behaviour in question, two of the most frequently used measures are to record either the number of times the behaviour occurs during a certain time (frequency), or the length of time that the behaviour lasts (duration) (cf. Grant and Evans, 1994).

Recording behaviour is really important in Behaviour Analysis (more on this throughout the book). Recording Jack's behaviour for ten days before the intervention gave me information before the programme started (the baseline data). Later on I was able to compare the baseline data with the data collected during the intervention and this enabled me to decide whether or not the intervention was going in the right direction.

Keeping data

Keeping data throughout the intervention is essential for monitoring your child's progress. This can sound intimidating, but in some interventions it can be as straightforward as noting down a tick for 'correct' and a cross for 'incorrect' on a simple table. Dates and procedures should be noted for each session as it's easy to forget details when working on a number of behaviours. After the teaching exercise, you record the numbers of correctly performed behaviours (e.g., 6 behaviours correct out of 10 opportunities = 60% correct). You might, for example, put the value of 60% onto a simple graph that shows other daily performances of the same skill that is being taught. You would use this graph as a kind of data diary.

I decided to record the duration of Jack's screaming, and began to take a note of how long Jack screamed (wanting Cola) on return from school (always have a pencil and paper at hand during Behaviour Analysis sessions). I then transferred the results onto a simple graph (see Chapter 5). This gave me the opportunity to see clearly the extent of the problem and later on it was used to indicate whether the programme was working.

On another occasion I was teaching Jack to distinguish between different shapes. We started simply with a card cut out in the shape of a square. He was to say 'square' when I showed it to him. Once he was obtaining at least 80% correct responses over three teaching sessions, it was easy to conclude that the skill was in place. The results collected were the signposts for any further steps in the development of the intervention. Thus, for example, if Jack had consistently failed to master the skill (as indicated by a consistently low score being recorded for each session), then I would have had to review my procedures. This is what behaviour analysts call data-based decision-making. Decisions about your intervention depend on your data, not on the latest fad or fashion, or a gut feeling that you may have. If your data shows that an intervention is not working, you change the intervention! In Jack's case this could have meant breaking down the behaviour he had to acquire into smaller, more manageable steps, or reconsidering the reinforcers I was using (see below). This is where the advice of a trained behaviour analyst is really essential. It's not a failure to go back; if reviewing 'disappointing' data lets you think round a problem, then you're acquiring new skills you can apply to other situations. It also takes the pressure off both you and your child when you can see the problem as a task to be analysed rather than someone's 'fault'.

Learning our ABCs

Earlier when I talked about the precision involved in defining Jack's screaming behaviour I omitted to talk about two other things that complete the picture. These two things together with his behaviour make up what behaviour analysts call the ABCs of Behaviour Analysis. The first thing you do when analysing a behaviour (abbreviated as 'B') is to identify the circumstances that need to be in place before the behaviour appears. The technical term for the circumstances that occasion the behaviour is 'Antecedent', hence the abbreviation 'A'. Once the behaviour has taken place there will be something that happens afterwards, a 'Consequence', and this is abbreviated as 'C'. When behaviour analysts look at any behaviour they always work with ABCs to determine what was the 'A', the 'B', and the 'C'. The ABC of Behaviour Analysis is also sometimes called the 'three-term contingency'. Yes, another technical term but this refers simply to what I have said already: if A is in place, then B occurs, and if B occurs then C follows it. When you get used to it you will find that this is a really neat way of understanding behaviour because it helps you to find ways to deal with it. For example, when I was teaching Jack to distinguish between different shapes my instruction 'Say square' and showing him the actual square shape together made up the antecedent. The problem for Jack was that he did not engage in the appropriate behaviour in the presence of this antecedent. My goal, then, was to ensure that he made the right response. Jack's response, saying the word 'Square', was deemed the appropriate behaviour, and my praise was the consequence for saying this word.

Antecedent → Behaviour → Consequence

'Say square' ⟶ 'Square' ⟶ 'Well done, Jack'

Figure 1.1

If, after training, Jack's behaviour did not occur in the way specified by my definition of the target behaviour, then I would have to look at either the antecedent or the consequence, or both, to see if I should change them in some way. My goal was for Jack to be successful in each new learning situation. If he was not successful, then I had to question my design of his learning environment. The three-term contingency is one of the main tenets in Applied Behaviour Analysis and you will hear much more about it in this and subsequent chapters.

Consequences

While some interventions are based on changing the antecedents of behaviour, most interventions that we will discuss here are based on changing consequences of behaviour. You may ask 'What does that mean?' Behaviour analysts have found that some consequences of behaviour make it more likely that we do the same thing again (called reinforcers), other consequences make it less likely that we repeat the behaviour (called punishers). We will concentrate here on reinforcers for a number of reasons. First, reinforcers are much more fun, and second, if we can get our child to behave appropriately most of the time that means that we don't need to stop him from behaving inappropriately so often. So, we use 'reinforcement' most often in Applied Behaviour Analysis with our children.

I looked up the dictionary definition of 'reinforce', and it says: to reinforce is 'to strengthen by additional assistance, material, or support, to make stronger or more pronounced'. This is pretty much how a behaviour analyst would define 'reinforcement'. If you supply a consequence for a child's behaviour and it makes that behaviour more likely to happen again in the future, behaviour analysts would consider this consequence a reinforcer. Therefore, in the application of Behaviour Analysis you use reinforcers if you want to increase the future occurrence of a desirable behaviour. Of course it is important that the behaviours that are reinforced are those that are important for the child and that they will help increase his social, emotional, and intellectual development and well-being.

Types of reinforcement

There are two types of reinforcement, positive and negative. It can be a bit confusing, since both types of reinforcement strengthen behaviour. The difference is that if you want to use positive reinforcement you will add (+) something; usually this is something the child likes such as praise, hugs, etc. If a behaviour is negatively reinforced, it means that the behaviour is followed by the removal of something (-), usually something that is not so nice, like the demand to do homework. Because negative reinforcement is often based on the removal of something that is not so pleasant it is also often called avoidance learning, or escape learning (Grant and Evans, 1994).

Using Applied Behaviour Analysis we usually concentrate on positive reinforcement. It is, however, important to understand negative reinforcement because all too often the undesired behaviours that a child displays (behavioural excesses) are unintentionally negatively reinforced. In other words, the child has learned that he can avoid a demand by behaving in a certain way, for example, a child may throw a temper tantrum when he is asked to tidy his room. When parents are faced with this kind of situation, it does not seem worth the hassle and it is usually much easier to give up on the request for a tidy room. Usually the child will then stop the tantrum. However, he may have learned: If I want to avoid tidying my room, all I have to do is to throw a temper tantrum. Because we are often faced with dealing with temper tantrums in our children, it is important to understand negative reinforcement. But now, let's get back to positive reinforcement.

For any type of reinforcement to be effective, it must be accurately timed and delivered promptly following the desired behaviour. Your child must know what exactly it is you are so pleased about. If your reinforcer is badly timed or late, this can lead to confusion, and in fact you may end up reinforcing the wrong thing. Say, for example, your child is not speaking and you are working on teaching him a word. You have set up a teaching programme and he is beginning to make some appropriate sounds and immediately afterwards he starts stimming by hand flapping. You must be very precise with the timing of the reinforcer to ensure that you don't reinforce the inappropriate behaviour, hand flapping, instead of the target behaviour, speaking.

A tip to note when delivering praise as a reinforcer: remember initially to use descriptive language in your statements to help clarify what is being reinforced, for example, say 'good looking' instead of 'good boy, well done' if you are trying to reinforce eye contact. In a vague statement like the latter, there is more chance of the child missing the message and not fully grasping what it is he has done 'right'. As the child becomes more competent the feedback can take on a more naturalistic form.

Types of reinforcers

Just as there are two types of reinforcement (positive and negative), so there are two types of reinforcers, primary and secondary. A primary reinforcer can be a 'tangible' reward such as food or drink. It is something that is naturally reinforcing, and may have biological importance. The second type are secondary reinforcers. Secondary reinforcers are usually more abstract, such as praise and hugs and are things that may have become more reinforcing by being paired with a primary reinforcer. For example, if you have been using chocolate buttons (primary reinforcer) with your child, together with praise, then in time you can probably use praise alone, as it will have become a secondary reinforcer. This is a particularly important point to learn if your child currently is not responding to praise, because it means that you can actually teach him to respond to praise appropriately. Many of us working with our children find praise, hugs, or tickles serve well as reinforcers, and indeed these reinforcers are quite natural, universal, and convenient (you always have them with you!).

Describing reinforcers

In practical terms, is there any one thing that should be used as reinforcer? It is impossible for me to answer that question, save to give some examples of the things we have successfully used with James. This is because every child is an individual with different likes and dislikes, so, in fact, what 'works' for one will not necessarily 'work' for another child.

Typically, however, reinforcers are perceived as positive objects or activities, such as sweets, food, videos, or favourite toys. A tip when using edible reinforcers is to keep them as small as you can get away with, so that they don't become distracting or interrupt the flow of work. Besides, using sweets as reinforcers has health implications, in particular for your child's teeth. The goal is to teach the child to respond to natural and social reinforcers.

Reinforcers may be quite unusual and you may even consider using 'obsessive favourites' that then become rewards and hugely motivating in terms of the child's behaviour and learning. I can give you an unusual example of something that 'worked' well as a reinforcer for our son James. He had just begun to master some basic elements of verbal imitation, simple sounds only. We were, of course, continually reinforcing all such sounds with praise, hugs etc. (all of which James enjoys, but remember your child may not). While out walking one day, James kept pulling at my hand to let him stamp on drain coverings at the side of the road off the footpath. I realised quite quickly that this was very enjoyable for him, and so I began to require a particular behaviour (copying of a sound) from him, before providing the reinforcer (allowing him to walk on the drains). In other words, I deliberately arranged my ABCs shown in Figure 1.2.

I got more verbal imitation from him on that short walk up the road than I had in many previous attempts in other circumstances and he was having fun. I use this example to demonstrate that you have to be sensitive to your child's desires (however odd they may appear to be from time to time), and creative in your approach to finding reinforcers.

Antecedent ⟶ Behaviour ⟶ Consequence

My instruction for him to make a particular sound	⟶	His behaviour of copying that sound	⟶	Being allowed to stamp on a drain covering

Figure 1.2

Selecting and finding reinforcers

So how do you decide which things are going to serve as reinforcers for your child? Finding reinforcers can be time consuming, indeed all consuming for some who are always on the look out for novel, exciting, and unusual toys and objects which may interest their children.

One of the most obvious methods for selecting potential reinforcers is simply to observe your child. Record the kinds of activities your child likes the most. The things a person does most of the time are probably the most reinforcing. Although this is not a terribly accurate procedure, it may be helpful. Talk to others who care for him/her (perhaps in different settings, such as school or playgroup). You could try presenting your child with two items and see which one is chosen. The one s/he chooses should work as a better reinforcer.

Remember too, what may be reinforcing one day, may not be so the next. You really need to do a reinforcer assessment frequently, at least once a week and probably more often. Choice itself can be a powerful reinforcer. One way to arrange learning is to let the child choose both the task and the reinforcers. Another way to make reinforcers more potent is to eliminate these items from the rest of your child's life from time to time. For example, we kept James off chocolate for a while and reserved it as a reinforcer for work time. If play-time with particular toys is used as reinforcer, these toys should be kept in a closed box where access is restricted. If the child can play with these toys just any old time, they will lose their potency as reinforcers.

Reinforcement in day-to-day life: An example

Some time ago, James persisted in taking off his shoes and socks in the car during journeys. Every time we stopped somewhere, and I wanted to get James out from the back seat his socks and shoes would be off. I realised that I had inadvertently been reinforcing this behaviour by commenting on it (usually jokingly) and sometimes even tickling his feet. Of course James was enjoying all this, and so the removing of socks and shoes continued. Once I realised that my response was inadvertently reinforcing this 'problem behaviour', I changed what I did. With absolutely no comment, smiles, and certainly nothing that could be construed as a tickle, I would calmly put his socks and shoes back on and lead him from the car. The 'problem' behaviour ceased after about eight days.

I had to be sure always to respond in this way. If I reverted sometimes to comments or tickles that would have provided something we have learned to call intermittent reinforcement. Intermittent reinforcement is more powerful than continuous reinforcement and usually results in behaviour that is more resistant to change. If the child doesn't always know whether the reinforcer is coming next time, s/he is more likely to keep trying 'just in case'. It's a bit like the difference between a coin-operated snack vending machine (continuous reinforcement: every time you insert a coin, you get a chocolate bar) and a slot machine (which provides random pay outs on an intermittent basis), and we all know how compulsively addictive slot machines can be.

In concluding this section on reinforcement I quote an old adage to sum up, 'A reinforcer is only a reinforcer if it reinforces' – think about it!

How I plan an intervention

The range of interventions can seem endless when you first begin learning about Behaviour Analysis. Every time you think you have understood an intervention, the behaviour analysts you are working with will probably come up with another possibility. The important thing here is not to learn them all off by heart, but to keep an open mind, learn, and use your imagination. After all, any intervention is only as good as the change it achieves with your child.

In most cases the behaviour that you want to teach is broken down into small steps. Each step is then taught until the child carries it out readily. Prompts are sometimes needed at the beginning of a new task to get the child started; for example, I used a prompt such as gentle physical guidance when Jack was learning how to use a pencil. I began by putting my hand over his to guide him and give him the confidence to try himself. Then, over time, I gradually used less and less pressure on his hand so he was continuing himself. This procedure is called 'fading'. Applied Behaviour Analysis has developed a multitude of procedures; they all have different names that can be difficult to remember. However, once you have used a procedure successfully, it becomes much easier to recall scientific jargon. Sometimes you may even see the point in using jargon, for example, when you are trying to explain a procedure to another parent.

Arranging the learning environment

Before you start work you will have to think about how to arrange the environment in which you are going to teach your child. We have already seen that Behaviour Analysis can be applied in any situation; for example, during a walk James learned to improve his speech, in the car he learned to keep his shoes on. Later we will see how, in the kitchen Jack learned to ask properly for a drink and how, in his living room, Colin learned to keep eye contact.

However, many parents will probably begin behaviour analytic work with their child in a more formal setting. Arranging a table and chairs in a relatively quite room is often the best way to ensure that your child and you can concentrate on the task in hand during the early stages of your work. In this situation skills can be broken down into small steps and, using one-to-one teaching, you and your child can practise the required behaviours as often as necessary. This kind of teaching has been called 'discrete trials' and it was probably the first teaching method I used when starting an Applied Behaviour Analysis programme with my son Colin. Discrete trials are really only a more intensive extension of methods most of us use with our other children; for example, teaching tables or spellings, where we 'rehearse' the correct response a number of times to make sure the child has a good understanding of the task.

Once you have decided which behaviours you want to teach, each 'step' is consistently taught and recorded in a series of practice runs, called 'trials'. This structured method of teaching can be used to train behaviours extending from simple attending skills to language concepts. Although it's hard work, it should also be made as much fun as possible – many parents use games and songs when teaching in trials.

Starting work

I noticed that Colin's eye contact was poor, and chose this as a target behaviour in an early programme that we had worked out together with a trained behaviour analyst (see Chapter 4 for a description of many of the other things we taught Colin). The target behaviour had to be carefully defined: 'eye contact' could vary from a fleeting sideways glance to a rigid, unblinking stare. It was essential that we were as precise as possible about our aims, such as aiming for eye contact for two seconds. You should also be as brief and as consistent in your instructions as possible. 'Look at me' is better than 'OK, right, now I want you to look at me – come on now, look at mum'. Once Colin was responding accurately to 'Look at me', then I could gradually become more flexible with the request. It's also a good idea to move away from primary reinforcers such as sweets as quickly as possible. There is sometimes a perception that in discrete trials the child is being force-fed Smarties® to produce responses in rigid, stressful situations. This just wouldn't happen in any teaching situation where Behaviour Analysis was being properly applied. Making learning enjoyable is part of this; if 'work' is associated with positive reinforcement, then children don't have problems with doing it.

So how do discrete trials work in practice? The first 'trial' consisted of simply sitting in front of Colin, in a quiet, familiar room, and saying 'Look at me' (Antecedent). Each time Colin looked at me (Behaviour) he received a suitable reinforcer, such as a Smartie® and praise (Consequence). If he did not look at me, I gently turned his face to obtain eye contact, saying 'this is looking at me'; this is referred to as a prompt. Eventually he began looking at me without the physical prompt. I repeated this simple ABC sequence a number of times and each time I noted down whether or not there was a correct response or a prompted response. I used sessions of five or ten instructions as it made calculating '% correct' a lot easier.

Shaping

Shaping is a procedure that is used in nearly all programmes. In behaviour analytic jargon we say that it is the differential reinforcement of successive approximations of a target behaviour until that target behaviour is exhibited by the individual. I see it in more everyday terms: 'Shaping' is helping a child grow more and more skilled in ways that will be useful to him now, or later in life. The general procedure involves breaking a complex task down into small units and reinforcing successful completion of each unit. When each unit is learned the next one is added and this continues until the child can perform successfully all of the units in the correct sequence.

Every day adults shape children in a process parents call child rearing and teachers call education! Mind you, not all parents and teachers 'shape' children in ways that maximise their learning and even good ones don't always do it consistently. But most loving parents and teachers are more or less shaping their charges as effectively as they can most of the time.

My son, Eoin, is 11 and has Asperger's Syndrome and moderate language difficulties. He has always had difficulty with abstract language and with mathematics. In fact, he had considerable difficulty with the concept of money. Before we started work with him he could not manage or count money, he could only buy an item in the shop if we sent him with a written note and we trusted the shop assistant to take only the correct money. I started by teaching him to identify the different coins. When he could name the different coins reliably, we worked on arranging them in a line from least to greatest value: 1p, 2p, 5p, 10p, 20p, 50p, £1. Once this was mastered, we started work on adding the value of the coins. Although he had learned to add units, tens and hundreds in school he could not add the coins because he did not write the values of the coins under each other correctly. We had been working on white unlined paper (silly me!). The behaviour analyst advised me to get horizontally-lined paper, to get Eoin to make the figures bigger, and to put in vertical guiding lines to keep the pence under the pence, the tens under the tens and so on. This worked very well. We started with simple sums: add 2p + 5p etc. and when this was mastered, went on to 2p + 5p + 5p. At the end he was able to count the entire content of his money box: £28.73 with no difficulty whatsoever.

This example shows how shaping can be used to move from a situation where the child is unable to do something to being able to cope quite well. When we started, Eoin could not even identify the various coins. The shaping process guided him through counting several coins in one denomination, to counting all coins in all denominations.

Extinction

Extinction of behaviour is a phenomenon that can be harnessed when you need to reduce a problem behaviour. Extinction occurs when a behaviour that has been previously reinforced no longer results in the reinforcing consequence and, therefore, eventually stops occurring. In other words, if someone experiences a benefit from a behaviour even occasionally, they may continue to engage in that behaviour until there is no longer a benefit for them in it. For example, when Eoin was a toddler we used to stay with my parents in Bray and over many visits he became enamoured of the DART (Dublin Area Rapid Transport), a train that travelled into the city. If ever you asked Eoin what he would like to do, he would say, 'See the train'. This was fine in small doses but one summer, when we ended up spending half the day at the level crossing in Bray waiting for the train to leave the station, we knew it was time to call it a day. The alternative to staying was tantrums and Eoin being taken away kicking and screaming, to the beach or funfair or wherever.

As we were going to be there for a month and nobody could make plans for excursions for the rest of the family (we were spending so much of the day in the station) we decided to extinguish the behaviour. At least we decided to extinguish the obsessive, relentless aspect that was making everybody miserable. We arranged a morning excursion but told Eoin we would bring him to the train immediately after breakfast and again at lunch and bedtime. After breakfast off we set for the station and all went well until we took him away after seeing the train leave. There was a tantrum but we stuck to our plans. At lunch time the same thing happened again. There were also tantrums at times during the day (especially if he was bored). It was noticeable that the tantrums declined considerably after the first day though.

With extinction the normal course of action would be to wait until the child had completely adjusted to the new situation (I think) but we did not feel we could do this. (We were afraid of being there all holiday!) After a few days of three visits to the train station a day we cut these back to morning and night only. Again there were tantrums but these also faded in duration and intensity over the next week, until he accepted the new arrangements. At that point we did not want to alter things further: we knew that watching trains was a great interest of his, so were happy to bring him twice daily. In this example the behaviour was not extinguished completely; it did not need to be – but the aspect of it that was ruining the holiday for everyone was altered for the better.

Another example of extinction was the work we did with Jack's screaming for Cola when he returned home from school. The intervention I used to stop Jack from screaming was as follows: After telling Jack there was no Cola (I had no Cola in the house that day. It made it much easier for me to be consistent), I totally ignored him when he started to scream. In other words, I did not give him what he usually got. On the first day he screamed for 15 minutes; we then went up to his nannie's, and she gave him a bottle with about an inch of Cola in it, so he was not totally deprived of his favourite drink. The next day his screaming lasted 30 minutes. Behaviour Analysts have called this an 'extinction burst' and have found that it is part of the pattern to be expected when behaviour is successfully put on extinction. That is, it gets worse before it gets better. When Jack's screaming behaviour followed this expected pattern I knew we were going in the right direction. The following day he came in from school, and the tantrum lasted only five minutes. Eventually his tantrums disappeared. During the programme, we also taught Jack how to ask appropriately if he wanted something, thereby replacing the inappropriate behaviour with appropriate behaviour.

Generalisation

It is important that during a programme you concentrate on making new skills occur in a variety of everyday situations. This is called preparing for 'generalisation'. Many children with autism have a problem with generalisation. Behaviours acquired in one situation may not appear elsewhere. For example, a child who is taught to complete a shape-sorting task at home may not do this at an assessment session with a psychologist. Generalising skills should be part of any competent individual teaching programme. When a skill is being taught, then it should be taught across a wide variety of situations – at different times, in different rooms (or places), with as many people as possible. For example, when Jack had learned to ask appropriately for Cola I taught him to ask appropriately for all sorts of other things throughout the day. Another example of generalisation was when Jack was learning to distinguish between different shapes. As Jack began to learn what a square was, he responded correctly more often and I pointed out squares at every opportunity, and made it fun by saying: 'The box is square', 'Look at the square window'.

If you were teaching a child the difference between red and blue, you may initially use blocks, or coloured cards, in a series of trials; that's an important skill, but it's only the beginning. Your child could then be encouraged to pick out red and blue from pictures, then everyday objects, with other family members and friends joining in. This is all part of how children generalise, and it can be trained both in 'trials' and in everyday situations through incidental learning. For instance, you could make an exaggerated effort to point out red or blue cars when out for a walk, or ask him to indicate his choice of a red or blue cup when he wants a drink. Most of us do this in a casual way with all small children, but especially for children with autism, every teaching opportunity counts. You should actively create opportunities to practise newly developing skills it in different situations. Encourage children to take charge of the learning process; the more the programme is child-led the better.

Eye contact can be 'taught' in a variety of trials, but it's likely to be most natural when it's used in normal, everyday situations as well. Teaching a child to make definite eye contact when talking directly to you, or when asking or signing for a drink or a biscuit, is a very important way to practise the skill. If such behaviour is reinforced, with your attention, or the requested drink or snack, then it's more likely to reappear. Learning in incidental situations, at the kitchen table, in the supermarket, on holiday, on the bus, is a substantial part of helping your child appropriately use the skills you've both worked so hard to put in place.

Summary

As someone who progressed over a few weeks from thinking ABA was a Swedish pop group, to discussing the merits of primary reinforcers in different teaching formats, I ask you not to be discouraged at any lack of success in the early stages, but to stick with it. This has made a huge difference to our children and the whole family, helping us cope with behaviour that is challenging us every day. Using Applied Behaviour Analysis changed the way we looked at learning and teaching. It helped us to see everyday events as opportunities to widen our children's horizons.

References

Grant, L. and Evans, A. (1994) *Principles of Behavior Analysis.* New York: HarperCollins.

CHAPTER 2

Applied Behaviour Analysis
The Therapy of Choice

Ken P. Kerr

Chapter 1 has highlighted the key features of Applied Behaviour Analysis (ABA) as written and experienced by parent members of PEAT. This chapter introduces key issues in relation to research carried out by international behaviour analysts in the area of autism. The aim of this chapter is to present findings from the academic literature in a clear and accessible way. From this, parents and interested parties will see that Applied Behaviour Analysis is indeed the therapy of choice. The importance of parent/family input, following specialised training, within the ABA treatment paradigm is emphasised. Overall this chapter aims to introduce parents to many of the key issues in terms of research and criteria for effective treatment.

What is autism?

The Autistic Spectrum Disorder (ASD) as listed in the DSM-IV (American Psychiatric Association, 1994) is considered a pervasive developmental disability. The disorder is usually diagnosed on the strength of extensive direct behavioural observation of the child and interviews with parents and family members. However, the disorder remains difficult to assess (Jordan, Jones and Murray, 1998). Generally, children are diagnosed with ASD if a number of excesses and deficits in behaviour are apparent before the age of three years. These excesses and deficits, which vary from child to child, usually occur in social interaction, language, social communication, symbolic or imaginative play, and repetitive and stereotyped patterns of behaviour. Although the exact cause is unknown, it is widely felt that the disorder is biological, although non-specific in origin; it is thought that brain development is affected. The symptoms are three to four times more likely to be seen in boys than girls, and span all geographical, cultural and social backgrounds.

Due to the difficulty in obtaining a diagnosis it is not surprising that the exact number of people on the autistic spectrum is hard to estimate. Discrepancies in the estimated prevalence have been acknowledged by many authors (see Jordan, Jones and Murray, 1998). In the USA Maurice, Green, and Luce (1996), for example, cite an incidence rate of 5–15 per 10, 000, while The National Autistic Society (NAS, 1997) provides an estimate of 91 per 10, 000 in the U.K. It should be noted that the NAS estimate stems from a summary of research over the last 50 years and relates to the number of people for the *entire* spectrum of disorders, not specific sub-groups.

What does the research tell us?

This section reviews major pieces of research, which show that early intensive behavioural treatment offers a favourable outcome for children with autism. It is argued that although the Autistic Spectrum Disorder may have a biological cause it is wrong to think that there is nothing that can be done (see Cambridge Centre for Behavioural Studies, 1999). The importance of age as a predictor of success is highlighted, although research that shows that older children can also benefit significantly from ABA is also reviewed.

The University of California, Los Angeles (UCLA) Young Autism Project (Lovaas, 1987) utilised an early intensive behavioural treatment approach for children with autism. They measured the intellectual and adaptive functioning when assessing children's ability to cope with the everyday environment. All children (aged under 40 months if non-verbal or under 46 months if verbal) were tested on a wide range of pre-treatment variables including being non-verbal, rejection of adults, lack of toilet training, gross inattention, tantrums, absence of toy play, self-stimulation, and absence of peer play. A diagnosis of autism and subsequent evaluation of progress was also performed by professionals not involved in the study to ensure impartiality.

One group of 19 children was exposed to the early behavioural intervention programme for 2 years. These children received 40 hours per week of intensive one-to-one behavioural intervention. A second group of 19 children, Control group 1, was exposed to a minimal behavioural treatment for 10 hours per week along with a traditional mixture of programmes (similar to that delivered in Special Education classes). Another group of 21 children, Control group 2, was exposed to a programme of a mixture of treatments by agencies external to the staff involved in the delivery of early behavioural intervention.

Results from this study show clear differentiation between the development of children in the behavioural intervention group compared to both the control groups. Of the intensive one-to-one group, 47% (9 children) achieved NORMAL educational and intellectual functioning compared to 2.5% of the children in the combined control groups. Average IQ gains of 20 points were recorded for children in the intensive behavioural treatment group. Similar gains were not recorded for children in the control groups. Of the intensive one-to-one group, 42% who did not achieve normal functioning, still made significant gains. The remaining 11% of the children made limited gains.

A follow-up study assessed children from the intensive behavioural treatment group and children from one of the control groups at a mean age of 11.5 years (McEachin, Smith and Lovaas, 1993). This study was designed to see whether the improved quality of life for individuals with autism and their families was comprehensive and if the changes in IQ and adaptive functioning endured (see Perry, Cohen and DeCarlo, 1995 for further discussion of children maintaining significant gains). An extensive test battery was administered to the nine children in the behavioural treatment group who had been classed as normal functioning in the 1987 study. The tests measured potential deficits in areas such as:

- idiosyncratic thought patterns, mannerisms, and interests
- lack of close relationships with family and friends
- difficulty in getting along with people
- relative weaknesses in certain areas of cognitive functioning, such as abstract reasoning
- not working up to ability in school
- flatness of affect
- absence or peculiarity in sense of humour (McEachin *et al.*, 1993, p.360).

The tests also measured potential strengths such as:

- normal intellectual functioning
- good relationships with family members
- ability to function independently
- appropriate use of leisure time
- adequate socialisation with peers (McEachin *et al.*, 1993, p.360).

It was found that eight out of the nine children (42% of the original sample of 19 children) showed normal educational and intellectual functioning and were '…indistinguishable from average children on tests of intelligence and adaptive behaviour' (McEachin *et al.*, 1993, p.359). The progress of seven of these children was reviewed when they were young adults (see London Early Autism Project, 1999):

> 'In terms of their independent functioning, four had gone to college, one had graduated from high school, and one had not graduated. Three had regular jobs, one was self-employed, one was still in college, and one was unemployed … All said they had close friends. In terms of problems with peers, two felt they had problems with their temper and one felt that they had a problem of being shy, and three said that they had no problems at all. In terms of romance, one was married, three had current boyfriends or girlfriends, one had a girlfriend or boyfriend in the past, two had no current boyfriend or girlfriend, and all of them wanted to get married.' (p.7)

These findings are testament to the potential long-term positive outcome of behavioural programmes with children with autism. Many more studies lend support to the statement that Applied Behaviour Analysis offers the best outcomes for children diagnosed with autism. Anderson, Campbell, and Cannon (1994), for example, provided clinic- (integrated class settings) and home-based service to pre-school children. Out of the 26 children who participated for one year or longer, 14 children (54%) progressed to regular kindergarten education (some with classroom assistants), 2 children (8%) remained in a resource room, and 10 children (38%) went to segregated private schools.

Other findings supporting the efficacy of intensive behavioural intervention include research by Birnbrauer and Leach (1993). They provided intensive early behavioural intervention for nine children with autism. At the end of a two-year treatment programme four out of the nine children had made substantial gains in IQ, language, and adaptive behaviour tests. One of the five children in the control group who received no intensive behavioural treatment showed substantial gains in adaptive behaviour and language. None of the children in the control group showed improvements in intellectual functioning.

In the Douglass Developmental Disabilities Centre (Rutgers University, New Jersey) behavioural provision is offered in an integrated setting. Researchers there tested intelligence and language performance of nine pre-school children with autism when they first entered the programme and again one year later. These children gained 19 IQ points and 8 language performance points over the year (Harris and Handlemann, 1994).

Despite the extensive range of studies utilising early intensive behavioural treatment most of them are based on common basic key elements. It is to these that we now turn.

Criteria for effective treatment

It is commonly agreed that key elements for successful treatment include the timing of behavioural intervention (i.e., the age of the child), the intensity of the treatment (e.g., one-to-one treatment and the number of teaching hours per week), continuity between service providers, and parental involvement (Harris and Weiss, 1998; Lovaas, 1993a, 1996; Simeonnson, Olley and Rosenthal, 1987; Smith, 1993).

The timing of behavioural treatment

Researchers from the Princeton Child Development Institute (PCDI) compared the treatment outcomes of nine children who received behavioural treatment before they were sixty months old with those of nine children who underwent the same program after sixty months (Fenske, Zalenski, Krantz and McClannahan, 1985). Results suggested that the age of children was related to positive outcome. That is, six children (67%) under sixty months achieved positive outcomes (i.e., they lived at home and were enrolled in public school on a full time basis) compared to one of the children (11%) in the older group.

Despite the limited sample size these results offer some support to the view that early behavioural intervention is advantageous. This does not mean that older children do not benefit from behavioural programmes. A preliminary study by Eikeseth, Jahr, and Eldevik (1997) assessed the effectiveness of a behavioural intervention for children aged four to seven. Although the study is ongoing, the results suggest that while the optimum age for starting behaviour analytic treatment is younger, children from the four- to seven-year age group also benefit significantly from intensive treatment.

The intensity of the treatment

Whilst more research is required into intensity of treatment, it appears that ten hours of treatment per week may not differ from no treatment. Twenty hours may produce modest gains (Anderson et al., 1987), and as much as 40 hours may be required to produce major improvements (Lovaas, 1987; see Smith, 1993 for further discussion). Parents should realise, however, that it is not the time element alone that critically determines outcome. The quality of teaching and the number of learning opportunities presented also determines outcome. Recently, research generated through the use of Precision Teaching has shown that children with autism can accelerate their learning (see Lindsley, 1992, for a general discussion of Precision Teaching). In presenting a higher number of learning opportunities children are taught to a fluency level based upon both the speed and accuracy of responding. Increased opportunity to practice the behaviour and to become fluent at particular skills through Precision Teaching may therefore also have a critical role to play in determining the outcome of an ABA programme.

ONE-TO-ONE INSTRUCTION

Initially the programme is delivered on a one-to-one basis. This is to ensure that the child acquires mastery of basic learning readiness skills that are required for later progression. At later stages the ratio of students to teachers is changed to reflect a typical classroom setting where children have mastered observational and group learning. Whilst the change in the instructional format may mean that a group context is created it is necessary to ensure that the educational planning is still geared towards the individual. Specific assessment of a child's progress is vital to ensure that the instructional format is meeting the needs of the individual.

Continuity between service providers

Behavioural programmes are not carried out in isolation. While benefiting from ABA at home the child may be enrolled in the school system, may be receiving speech therapy, or other forms of services and treatment. Consistency and continuity between all of these agencies is vitally important. The behavioural programme involves the implementation of scientifically based procedures ranging from simple reinforcement strategies (Chapter 1) to more complex procedures such as functional analysis (Chapter 3). Procedures are commonly designed in ways that allow the clear monitoring of progress and decisions are made based upon the data collected. However, school or other services that the child receives may not be structured in the same scientific way and it may be difficult to achieve consistency across programmes.

Behaviour analysts recognise the need for continuity. For example, with regard to preparing a child for entering school, behaviour analysts focus on achieving school-ready behaviours with a child, such as paying attention, turn taking, appropriate play, language, and pre-academic skills. Most children with autism need to be taught these skills explicitly to prepare them for participation and effective interaction in school settings. The ABA curriculum usually begins with teaching compliance, receptive language, imitation, pre-academics, and goes on to teach advanced learning strategies that result in the child 'learning how to learn' (see Chapter 5). ABA also deals with a range of difficulties that may hinder integration into school, such as sleep disturbances, separation difficulties, various types of behavioural regression, and expressive emotional problems. This does not mean that integration into mainstream school systems is a foregone conclusion, it means that mainstream schooling is put within reach for some children for whom it would not be contemplated otherwise. Regardless of the actual school the child is attending, an ABA-trained classroom aide should be employed initially to ensure a smooth transition from a home-based programme to a school programme.

Parental involvement

The importance of parents as teachers, advocates, and therapists for their children has long been recognised by behaviour analysts (Berkowitz and Graziano, 1972). Evidence for the need for full participation from parents came from early behavioural treatment of children with autism that was conducted within clinical settings. After treatment when these children returned to the institutions in which they lived they lost a wide range of the behaviours that they had acquired during treatment (Lovaas, Koegel, Simmons and Long, 1973). However, children who returned to the parental home maintained and improved upon their gains and research findings suggested that the behavioural treatment was valued highly by parents (Lovaas, 1993b).

Today most ABA programmes train and employ parents as co-therapists (Lovaas, 1987). There has been some debate about the rights and wrongs of this approach with contentions that such involvement and training is too stressful and intense for parents. However, the majority of researchers in the field have discovered that full parental involvement encourages continuity of services and generalisation of treatment results (Kerr, 2000). Peine (1969) found that 'It is possible that the best stress reduction takes place when a parent experiences some control over his or her children, and discovers that he or she can help the disadvantaged child grow and develop' (p.626). In fact, behaviour analysts contend that there is a moral justification for empowering parents with skills: '...it is the therapist's task to help the parent directly to be more effective in carrying out a parent's moral, ethical and legal obligation to care for his child' (Graziano, 1969, p.365). Legislation in Northern Ireland (Children (NI) Order 1995) and in Great Britain (Children Act 1989) reflects this with the call for parental participation and the identification of the need for partnership between agencies and parents.

The next question is, how does the aspiration to involve parents in the treatment of their children translate into practice?

Parent training: ABA is accessible

Behavioural parent training programmes teach parents and other family members skills that enable them to identify and promote occurrences of positive behaviour as well as deal with inappropriate behaviour in a way that will not compound the problem. In line with a preventative model of health care service (Holmes, 1998), behavioural parent training empowers those responsible for the child to take an active role in the treatment. How is this done? Callias (1994) highlights the skills that parents and other family members can acquire:

'Parents are usually taught how to define the problem that they are experiencing with their child in more precise behavioural terms, to observe accurately, to keep simple records as a baseline and for monitoring progress, to carry out a functional analysis, and to apply the range of techniques and principles that are relevant to effecting change.' (p.921)

PEAT has adopted a structure whereby trained behaviour analysts teach parents and caregivers the basic principles of Behaviour Analysis. Parents and other caregivers are taught the importance of clearly defining the target behaviour and are empowered with skills to make decisions based on the data collected. Participants on such training courses undergo monthly evaluation of performance to assess correspondence between their learning on the course and the actual application of behavioural principles. Further contact is provided when trained behaviour analysts visit each programme and take part in monthly team meetings. In this way, the team members (i.e., parents, professionals, and other caregivers) are encouraged to demonstrate that they are teaching effectively as only effective teaching will lead to substantial gains.

The important role of parents as advocates for behavioural training has often been recognised as a factor for ensuring the continuation of behavioural treatment programmes (Smith, 1993). Foxx (1996) called for behaviour analysts to consider themselves as behavioural ambassadors. The same title can aptly be bestowed upon parents involved in behavioural training programmes. Parents who undergo behavioural training prog-rammes are taught how to effectively translate behaviour analytic knowledge and apply it within their family setting. Also, parents who experience success in their role as teaching partners become envoys in the sense that they are in a better position to provide other parents with relevant first hand information on the effectiveness of ABA programmes. This new type of collaborative relationship is not, however, intended to usurp the role of professionals (see Mullen and Frea, 1996 for a discussion of a parent– professional consultation model). It is only through the input of a trained behaviour analyst that the quality of the ABA programme is assured.

Getting it straight

As early as 1981, DeMyer, Hingtgen, and Jackson reviewed the literature on autism in children and found that '...the overwhelming evidence suggests that the treatment of choice for maximal benefit to autistic children is a systematic, [intensive] behavioral/ educational approach' (p. 388). They went on to say '...the advantage of behavioral treatment programs remains impressive. They provide maximal opportunities for those autistic children with greatest potential, and, at the very least, furnish those children with the least potential the opportunity to acquire some significant behavioral skills' (p.435). These kinds of findings abound in ABA literature. We have also seen that ABA can be made accessible to parents through structured behavioural parent training. The question that could therefore be asked is 'Why is ABA and behavioural parent training not used routinely as the therapy of choice with children diagnosed with autism?'

Various reasons can be suggested as to why ABA is only recently being advocated to parents in Great Britain and Ireland. Most of the reasons can be tracked to a lack of knowledge about ABA. A little knowledge is a dangerous thing and parents and professionals are sometimes given inaccurate information. This is not unique to Great Britain and Ireland and this section will dispel some of these inaccuracies.

Inaccurate information

ABA promises a cure (Knott, 1995).

Accurate information

Behaviour analysts view autism as a series of excesses and deficits in the behavioural repertoire. As the cause of autism is unknown it is difficult to see how anyone would claim to be able to cure autism. Behaviour analysts do not make such claims. Instead, those misrepresenting Behaviour Analysis make this claim out of an apparent lack of understanding of behavioural principles. Behaviour is not cured; it can, however, be changed or managed. The amount of change possible can not be categorised into the pigeonholes of cured or not cured. The success of an ABA programme is relative to the starting point and is clearly shown through the data collected reflecting changes in behaviour. Meaningful change in behaviour is possible. The research literature does show that the behaviour typical of children with autism can be changed to leave some children in a position of being socially and educationally indistinguishable from their peers.

Inaccurate information

ABA is one of those fashionable new fads.

Accurate information

Behaviour analysts have been working in the area of autism for over 30 years. ABA effectiveness has been well documented during all this time. The sophistication of Behaviour Analysis has evolved greatly over the years and modern-day ABA has moved on from its early roots in behaviour modification in the 1960s (Walsh, 1997). Current breakthroughs and developments in the scientific knowledge base have lead to contemporary Behaviour Analysis providing one of the most researched and enduring treatment options for children diagnosed as autistic.

Inaccurate information

Current provision is 'appropriate'.

Accurate information

In many countries government departments have made commitments (financial and otherwise) to certain forms of service for children with autism. It seems that once an educational system is in place, it is in place for good, regardless of the evidence of effectiveness of alternative methods. ABA is 'appropriate' as it provides methods of education that have been tried and tested as consistently shown in peer-reviewed international journals. The reliance on data-driven procedures allows accountability which ensures that ABA is the most 'appropriate', that is, optimal form of education. Current provision that does not include ABA is therefore inadequate.

Inaccurate information

Behavioural teaching produces dependent learning styles (Knott, 1995).

Accurate information

In discussing one popular type of educational service, the TEACCH system (Treatment and Education of Autistic Communication Handicapped Children), Jordan *et al.* (1998) noted that 'TEACCH does not address the autism directly, but provides what might be called a 'prosthetic environment' for people with autism' (p.81).[1] What would happen if the prosthesis were removed? The answer given by a professional at a recent conference on learning disabilities in Northern Ireland was 'Would you dream of removing a guide dog from a blind person?'[2] Parents concerned with giving their children the best possible opportunities need to contrast systems like TEACCH that accept autism as a lifelong disability with systems that are designed to help to redress the balance between excesses and deficits in the behavioural repertoire of their child.

Behavioural teaching strives to produce independent learning styles. Key goals of ABA programmes are the achievement of self-management, independence, spontaneity, and creativity. The development of these skills will enable children to live their lives to the fullest potential. Catherine Maurice reflects the development of character and independence shown by her daughter who benefited from an intensive ABA programme:

> 'Anne-Marie is friendly and caring. She continues to make contact more easily with her peers and she is forming deeper relationships with them … Anne-Marie feels close to her teachers and is sharing more of her thoughts with them now … Anne-Marie is a co-operative, helpful group member who has learned to take her share of responsibility.' (Maurice *et al.* 1996, p.286)

Parents' reports of increased skills and expanded independence in their children clearly dispel any misguided notion that ABA produces dependent learning styles.

Inaccurate information
ABA uses aversive methods.

Accurate information
Aversive methods are *not* usually part of ABA teaching programmes. Instead, the focus of the teaching involves creating a highly motivated child due to the structuring of a warm nurturing environment using the principles of

---

1   The *Concise Oxford Dictionary* (1991) defines the word 'prosthetic' as 'an artificial part supplied to remedy a deficiency'.
2   It is unclear as to how representative this view would be for all professionals utilising TEACCH and it is unclear as to how similar TEACCH programmes in Northern Ireland are to those in North Carolina, USA. (See Paul Trehin's comments about importing some parts of TEACCH to Europe on http://www.unc.edu/depts/teacch/teacchn.htm#Section_0.1)

reinforcement (LaVigna and Donnellan, 1986). By arranging the antecedents of behaviour and delivering positive consequences it is possible to teach children how to enjoy the educational programme.

Both behaviour analysts and parents all too often experience these examples of misinformation. One commonality is that the individuals espousing these views generally have little, or no, formal training in Behaviour Analysis. Attending one workshop on behavioural principles does not qualify an individual to practice ABA or to make sweeping statements about its efficacy. Such misrepresentative views jeopardise the success of ABA programmes, and more importantly have a detrimental effect on the development of a child by denying the optimal form of education. In countering misrepresentation we allow parents access to the information which they can use to reach an informed decision as to the most effective type of educational provision for their child.

Reaching an informed decision

As parents we have to make decisions, take choices. These choices will have an impact on the lives of our children. This is true for all parents. Parents of children diagnosed with autism have to make additional decisions, choices about the treatment of their children. In this chapter it is argued that ABA should become the therapy of choice, because it has been proven to be the most effective treatment available. This is reflected in a parent's view which parents of the PEAT group have also come to hold:

'... it frightens me ... to wonder what she – and we – would be like if we had not chosen to pursue this course of action [ABA] for Rebecca. For now, we can only hope, continue to work as hard as we can on her behalf, and support, encourage, and protect her and each other.' (Harrington, 1996, p.371)

Another parent's comments show that ABA opens up many developmental avenues and fosters loving relationships between child and parent. This is a picture of a little boy who has discovered skills to help him blossom into a confident individual:

'We have also found that Brandon is very competitive ... He loves the attention and they [Brandon and his brother] enjoy their involvement with his program. It has been a real confidence booster for all the kids ... Brandon loves gymnastics, loves to swim, ride his bike, and run races. He is very co-ordinated ... Again, our focus has been to provide as many opportunities as possible. Also like most people, Brandon enjoys things he does well. These activities are great reinforcers and provide interesting and appropriate activities for his free time ... He is a very happy and productive young man. We are all proud of him.' (Kleinfeld-Hayes, 1996, p. 376)

Through the careful planning and implementation of early intensive behavioural programmes an environment can be designed to allow the successful development of children diagnosed as autistic. Whilst a certain amount of structure is required in implementing behavioural programmes, caregivers can acquire the flexibility and the skills to design individualised programmes. Parents and professionals therefore can become proactive in designing environments where positive consequences are delivered to allow success. The systematic work required is compatible, and indeed enhances, the developing emotional bonds between adult and child. Professionals and parents have a social and moral responsibility to implement effective procedures that improve the quality of life of the individuals in their charge.

Summary

Research employing ABA as the therapy of choice for children diagnosed with autism has continued to show that it offers the best outcomes in terms of educating children and enhancing life-skills. The result is that a significantly higher number of children lead more fulfilling lives than was previously thought possible. Those of you who want to explore the research data in more detail are encouraged to consult Matson *et al.* (1996) who refer to over 500 studies. These publications focus on a wide range of behaviours commonly experienced by parents of children with autism, including aberrant behaviour, social language, play skills, social interaction/initiation, and vocal language. In collaboration with trained behaviour analysts, parents can build on the success of these studies and become an important resource in organising and participating in therapeutic ABA programmes for the benefit of their children.

References

American Psychiatric Association (1994) *Diagnostic and Statistical Manual of Mental Disorders*, 4th edition Washington DC: American Psychiatric Association.

Anderson, S.R., Avery, D.L., Di Pietro, E.K., Edwards, G.L. and Christian, W.P. (1987) Intensive home-based early intervention with autistic children. *Education and Treatment of Children 10*, 352–366.

Anderson, S., Campbell, S. and Cannon, B.O. (1994) The May Center for Early Childhood Education. In S.L. Harris and J.S. Handleman (eds) *Preschool Education Programs for Children with Autism*. Austin: Pro-Ed.

Berkowitz, B.P. and Graziano, A.M. (1972) Training parents as behavior therapists: A review. *Behavior Research and Therapy, 10*, 297–317.

Birnbrauer, J.S. and Leach, D.J. (1993) The Murdoch early intervention program after 2 years. *Behavior Change, 10*, 63–74.

Callias, M. (1994) Parent training. In M. Rutter, E. Taylor and L. Hersov (eds) *Child and Adolescent Psychiatry: Modern Approaches* (pp.918–935) Oxford: Blackwell Scientific Publications.

Cambridge Centre for Behavioural Studies (1999) *Autism.* Retrieved from WWW page http://www.behavior.org/ on 15.5.99.

DeMyer, M.K., Hingtgen, J.N. and Jackson, R.K. (1981) Infantile autism reviewed: A decade of research. *Schizophrenia Bulletin, 7(3),* 388–451.

Eikeseth, J., Jahr, E. and Eldevik, S. (1997) *Intensive and Long Term Behavioural Treatment for Four to Seven Year Old Children with Autism: A One-Year Follow-Up.* Paper presented at PEACH Early Intervention Conference, 12th September.

Fenske, E.C., Zalenski, S., Krantz, P.J. and McClannahan, L.E. (1985) Age at intervention and treatment outcome for autistic children in a comprehensive intervention program. *Analysis and Intervention in Developmental Disabilities, 5,* 49–58.

Foxx, R.M. (1996) Translating the covenant: The behavior analyst as ambassador and translator. *Journal of Applied Behavior Analysis, 19,* 147–161.

Graziano, A.M. (1969) *Programmed Psychotherapy: A Behavioral Approach to Emotionally Disturbed Children.* Paper presented at the meeting of the Eastern Psychological Association, Boston.

Harrington, E. (1996) Rebecca's story. In Maurice, Green, and Luce (eds) *Behavioral Intervention for Young Children with Autism: A Manual for Parents and Professionals.* Austin, Texas: Pro-Ed.

Harris, S.L. and Handleman, J.S. (1994) (eds) *Preschool Education Programs for Children with Autism.* Austin: Pro-Ed.

Harris, S.L. and Weiss, M.J. (1998) *Right from the Start: Behavioral Intervention for Young Children with Autism. A Guide for Parents and Professionals.* Bethesda, MD: Woodbine House, Inc.

Holmes, Y. (1998) *The Role of Parents as Co-Therapists in Behavioural Programmes for Autistic Children.* Unpublished manuscript, University of Ulster.

Jordan, R., Jones, G. and Murray, D. (1998) *Educational Interventions for Children with Autism: A Literature Review of Recent and Current Research.* Final report to the Department for Education and Employment, June 1998.

Kerr, K.P. (2000) Managing children's behaviour in foster care. In G. Kelly and R. Gilligan (eds) *Issues in Foster Care.* London: Jessica Kingsley Publishers.

Kleinfeld-Hayes, C. (1996) Brandon's journey. In Maurice, Green, and Luce (eds) *Behavioral Intervention for Young Children with Autism: A Manual for Parents and Professionals* Austin, Texas: Pro-Ed.

Knott, F. (1995) *Approaches to Autism in the USA.* Winston Churchill Travelling Fellowship.

LaVigna, G.W. and Donnellan, A.M. (1986) *Alternatives to Punishment: Solving Behavior Problems with Non-Aversive Strategies.* New York: Irvington Publishers, Inc.

Lindsley, O.R. (1992) Precision teaching. Discoveries and effects. *Journal of Applied Behavior Analysis, 25,* 51–57.

London Early Autism Project. (1999) *Parent and Employee Orientation Manual and Policy Handbook.* London.

Lovaas, O.I (1987) Behavioral treatment and normal intellectual and educational functioning in autistic children. *Journal of Consulting and Clinical Psychology, 55,* 3–9.

Lovaas, O.I (1993a) *An open letter from O. I. Lovaas.* Retrieved from WWW Page http: //fox.nstn.ca/~zacktam/FEATbc/INFOSOURCES.html on 11.3.99.

Lovaas, O.I. (1993b) The development of a treatment-research project for developmentally disabled and autistic children. *Journal of Applied Behavior Analysis, 26,* 617–630.

Lovaas, O.I. (1996) *Criteria for Appropriate Treatments.* Reprinted in the *Proceedings from the Intensive Behavioural Intervention Conference,* Los Angeles, 1998.

Lovaas, O.I., Koegel, R.L., Simmons, J.Q. and Long, J.S. (1973) Some generalization and follow-up measures on autistic children in behavior therapy. *Journal of Applied Behavior Analysis, 6,* 131–166.

McEachin, S.J., Smith, T. and Lovaas, O.I. (1993) Long-term outcomes for children with autism who received early intensive behavioral treatment. *American Journal of Mental Retardation, 97(4),* 359–372.

Matson, J.L., Benavidez, D.A., Compton, L.S., Paclawskyj, T. and Baglio, C. (1996) Behavioral treatment of autistic persons: A review of research from 1980 to the present. *Research in Developmental Disabilities, 17,* 433–465.

Maurice, C., Green, G. and Luce, S.C. (eds) (1996) *Behavioral Intervention for Young Children with Autism: A Manual for Parents and Professionals.* Texas: Pro–Ed.

Mullen, K.B. and Frea, W.D. (1996) A parent-professional consultation model for functional analysis. In R.L. Koegel and L.K. Koegel (eds) *Teaching Children with Autism: Strategies for Initiating Positive Interactions and Improving Learning Opportunities.* Baltimore: Paul Brookes Publishing Company.

National Autistic Society (1997) *How Many People have Autistic Spectrum Disorders?* (Statistics Sheet 1) London: NAS.

Peine, H. (1969) *Programming the Home.* Paper presented at the meetings of the Rocky Mountains Psychological Association, Albuquerque, N.M.

Perry, R. Cohen, I. and DeCarlo, R. (1995) Case study: Deterioration, autism, and recovery in two siblings. *Journal of the American Academy of Child and Adolescent Psychiatry, 34(2),* 232–237.

Simeonnson, R.J., Olley, J.G. and Rosenthal, S.L. (1987) Early intervention for children with autism. In M.J. Guralnick and F.C. Bennett (eds) *The Effectiveness of Early Intervention for At-Risk and Handicapped Children.* New York: Plenum.

Smith, T. (1993) Autism. In Thomas R. Giles (ed) *Handbook of Effective Psychotherapy.* New York: Plenum Press.

Walsh, P. (1997) Bye-bye behaviour modification. In K. Dillenburger, M. O'Reilly, and M. Keenan (eds) *Advances in Behaviour Analysis.* Dublin: University of Dublin Press.

CHAPTER 3

Functional Assessment, Functional Analysis and Challenging Behaviour

Ian Taylor

A dominant theme in Applied Behaviour Analysis is the identification of effective methods to treat challenging behaviour (e.g., aggression, self-injury) in children with learning disabilities. There is now an abundance of effective treatment methods available for parents to use. Unfortunately, selecting the most appropriate intervention for each child continues to be a complex and often difficult process. Given their special needs, this is particularly true of children with autism. The development of functional assessment and functional analysis techniques makes this task much easier for parents. The primary purpose of these techniques is to identify the behaviour, its antecedents ('triggers') and consequences ('payoffs'). The explanation for any behaviour ultimately focuses on the identification of its antecedents and/or its consequences (see also Chapter 1). Technically speaking, behaviour is said to be a 'function of these antecedents or consequences'. In lay terms, we say the 'reason why' a behaviour occurs is because these antecedents or consequences are present.

Having identified the ABCs it is possible to determine the function of the problem behaviour; that is, you can make informed decisions about why the behaviour occurs. An intervention can then be developed which explicitly takes into account the function of the challenging behaviour. The aim of this chapter is to describe functional assessment and functional analysis techniques and inform parents how such techniques can be used to develop effective interventions suited to the needs of their child.

Applied Behaviour Analysis

Several carefully constructed studies have shown that early, intensive instruction using the methods of Applied Behaviour Analysis can result in dramatic improvements for children with autism (see Chapter 2; Lovaas, 1987; Lovaas and Smith, 1988, 1989). For example, behavioural training techniques have been shown to facilitate the development of social interaction (Gaylord-Ross, Haring, Breen and Pitts-Conway, 1984) and independent community living skills (Haring, Kennedy, Adams and Pitts-Conway, 1987). Similarly, important and effective behavioural change has occurred by decreasing challenging behaviours such as self-stimulation (Durand and Crimmins, 1988) and self-injury (Taylor, O'Reilly and Lancioni, 1996).

The need for enduring behavioural change

Despite the important advances of Applied Behaviour Analysis, many professionals and educators do not consider behavioural interventions to be completely successful. There is a perception that behavioural change can be brought about in training or educational settings but that such gains often do not persist (i.e., generalise or maintain) outside the training setting (Whitman, 1990). This is particularly true in terms of challenging behaviours such as aggression and self-injury that can be very resistant to change (Iwata, Dorsey, Slifer, Bauman and Richman, 1994).

Why is there a lack of enduring behavioural change?

One possible reason for the lack of generalisation and maintenance outside the training setting is that, until recently, interventions have tended to focus on the direction of behavioural change (i.e., decreasing the challenging behaviour) without considering the function of the behaviour (Lennox and Miltenberger, 1989).[1] For example, consider a young boy who screams on a regular basis. The child's mother and father may typically try to 'punish' the child's behaviour with a verbal reprimand. 'Punish' in this context is used as a technical term meaning to decrease the frequency of behaviour. As many parents know, however, it is difficult to be consistent with such a punishment regime. The child may learn very quickly that the screaming will not be punished if his/her mother and father are not in the room. Given that the reason (whatever it is) for the screaming still exists, any change using verbal

---

1   Such an approach is contradictory to the fundamental premise of Behaviour Analysis which describes behaviour primarily in terms of its function (Skinner, 1957).

reprimands to punish the screaming is likely to be short lived. In addition, during the period when the verbal reprimands are effective, other members of the family will have to put up with the screaming in the absence of the parents because the effects of punishment are unlikely to generalise beyond the child's mother and father.

The explanation for challenging behaviour should be determined before an intervention is developed

An alternative to the above scenario is for parents to determine the function of the behaviour and to develop an intervention that takes this into account. For example, what if the parents in the above example know that after the young boy screams he normally gains access to something (e.g., sweets, food, drink)? The child's mother and father may teach the child that he can get the drink (i.e., obtain this consequence) only when he asks for it properly (e.g., he holds out a hand and says 'I want'). At the same time the parents should teach the child that he doesn't get the drink in the presence of screaming (i.e., they withhold this consequence for his inappropriate behaviour). In this scenario, screaming should decrease (although there may be an initial increase in screaming – this is referred to as an extinction burst, see Chapter 1) and the absence of screaming should be maintained beyond the training setting. The reason for this enduring change is that not only the challenging behaviour has been decreased but, also, the boy has been taught an alternative and acceptable way to meet his needs; perhaps the new behaviour is also more efficient because it lessens the chance of confrontation.

Reasons for challenging behaviour

There are a number of reasons why a child with (or without) autism may engage in unacceptable and challenging behaviour (see Table 3.1; see O'Reilly, 1997 for a comprehensive review). For example, a child may engage in a temper tantrum to gain access to a preferred item (e.g., food or a particular toy). Alternatively, a child may exhibit challenging behaviour to obtain parental attention. With each of these two possibilities the tantrum is likely to be maintained by positive reinforcement. That is to say, parents may inadvertently reinforce the problem behaviour when they give the child the desired object or attention in an attempt to stop the tantrum.

Another possible reason for the occurrence of challenging behaviour is that it results in avoidance or escape from an aversive situation. In such a scenario, the challenging behaviour is maintained by negative reinforcement. For example, a parent may ask a child to do something that s/he is unwilling to do. If a temper tantrum occurs, the parent may respond with a verbal reprimand. If the child continues to tantrum, the parent is likely to withdraw the request in an attempt to stop it. While the tantrum may disappear for the moment the long-term result is that tantruming is likely to re-occur on each future occasion that the child is requested to do something that s/he finds aversive.

Table 3.1: Possible behavioural functions of challenging behaviour
(1) access to a material reinforcer (e.g., toy, food, drink; positive reinforcement)
(2) access to a social reinforcer (e.g., attention; positive reinforcement)
(3) avoidance of aversive stimulus (e.g., non compliance; negative reinforcement)
(4) physical stimulation (e.g., self-injury; automatic reinforcement)

Another explanation for the appearance of challenging behaviours can be traced to the role of self-stimulation (Repp, Singh, Olinger and Olson, 1990). It seems that some behaviours have *automatic reinforcement* properties (Skinner, 1982). This is particularly evident in many children with autism who frequently engage in hand flapping and other 'stimming'-type behaviours. If an alternative form of stimulation is not found then the reinforcing properties of this self-stimulatory behaviour are likely to maintain future 'stimming' behaviour. However, before we can conclude that self-stimulation explains an instance of challenging behaviour, the other possibilities outlined above should be eliminated first; fortunately these are often more amenable to subsequent behavioural intervention (Kennedy and Souza, 1995).

The above discussion provides some insight into why challenging behaviours occur. Without this understanding we would not be in a position to deal with various complications that arise in the management of these behaviours. There are occasions, for example, when behaviours that are topographically ('physically') similar occur for different reasons. That is to say, it has been shown that behaviours which appear similar (and by implication might be explained in the same way) are actually reinforced and maintained in different ways (see Lennox and Miltenberger, 1989); for example, head banging can serve to gain social attention or to avoid task completion. Such findings demonstrate the importance of determining the function of the challenging behaviour rather than merely relying on a description of it. To complicate the issue further, it is possible that the function of the challenging behaviour may change over time or indeed, that the challenging behaviour may fulfil a number of functions at any given time (Iwata, *et al.*, 1994). The upshot of these complications is that it is now recognised that individualised treatment programs should be tailored to meet the needs of each individual child (O'Reilly, 1997).

Risks of using an intervention without first determining the reason for the challenging behaviour

The selection of an intervention for a challenging behaviour that is not based on knowledge of the function of the behaviour may expose a child to a number of risks (Lennox and Miltenberger, 1989). One potential risk is that a child may be exposed to unnecessarily aversive and restrictive procedures. For example, a parent may typically punish unacceptable behaviour with a verbal reprimand or banishment to the bedroom. A second potential risk is that a child may be exposed to an ineffective intervention, thereby delaying the application of an effective treatment. Consider a young girl who engages in self-injurious behaviour with the result that she gains attention from her father. Typically the child's father may try to stop the self-injurious behaviour by reprimanding or restraining the child. This may seem like a punishment but if the self-injury is maintained by the father's attention (i.e., is a function of the father's attentive behaviour towards her), the father may be inadvertently reinforcing more self-injurious behaviour. In short, an intervention has been put in place by the child's father which is likely to increase (rather than decrease) the self-injurious behaviour.

Benefits of identifying behavioural antecedents and consequences

Knowledge of antecedents and consequences assists in the development of effective treatment procedures in a number of ways (Lennox and Miltenberger, 1989). First, identification of the reinforcing consequences of the challenging behaviour may suggest how to eliminate or prevent them; by removing or altering these reinforcing consequences the challenging behaviour may be prevented. Second, such pre-intervention assessments may allow parents to identify more efficient and socially appropriate behaviours that give their child access to consequences similar to those produced by the challenging behaviour (Carr and Durand, 1985; Durand and Carr, 1987). To illustrate the above possibilities, consider a young boy who engages in self-injurious behaviour. In some situations the boy may engage in self-injurious behaviour such as head banging and head hitting to obtain a toy or to get something to eat (i.e., access to a material reinforcer). In other situations the boy may engage in the same type of self-injurious behaviour to avoid complying with a parental request. In the absence of an analysis to determine the reason for the self-injurious behaviour, in both situations a parent may typically try to stop the self-injurious behaviour by giving a verbal reprimand. An alternative to the typical parental response is to develop interventions based on the reason for the challenging behaviour. In the first situation it might be appropriate for the parent to deny access to the drink and explain to the boy that he can't have the drink until he stops self-injuring and asks for it properly (e.g., he holds out a hand and says 'Please'). In the second situation, an appropriate intervention might be for the parent to teach the boy a more acceptable way to indicate reluctance to comply (e.g., the child shakes his head and says 'No').

Functional assessment and functional analysis techniques

While there are many behavioural treatment methods (Repp and Singh, 1990) the selection of the most effective intervention continues to be a complex and often difficult task (Lovaas and Favel, 1987). Particularly difficult is the identification of the antecedents and consequences that occasion and maintain very challenging behaviour. A thorough functional assessment and functional analysis must stand at the beginning of this process.

The term functional assessment has been used to describe a variety of systematic procedures to determine the antecedents that occasion and the consequences that maintain behaviour, including challenging behaviours (O'Reilly, 1997). Functional assessment typically involves a behavioural interview (see below). This is a process whereby the challenging behaviour is initially identified and defined by interviewing significant others (e.g., mother, father, teachers). In addition, possible antecedents and consequences are proposed by the interviewee(s). Following the behavioural interview, observation of the challenging behaviour occurs in the natural environment (i.e., where the behaviour has been described as problematic; see below). Assessment procedures may also involve the systematic manipulation of hypothesised (i.e., proposed) antecedents and consequences to confirm the suspicion that they do indeed occasion and maintain the challenging behaviour. This latter assessment is typically referred to as a functional analysis (O'Reilly, O'Kane and Taylor, 1994).

Functional assessment
Behavioural interview

A behaviour analyst usually carries out the behavioural interview. However, you can begin to assess your child's behaviour yourself if you try and answer the kind of questions s/he would ask you (see Table 3.2).

These kind of questions assist in identifying the antecedents and consequences occasioning and maintaining the challenging behaviour. However, although the behavioural interview is a good starting point, its usefulness is limited. Perhaps the major limitation of a behavioural interview is that there is no direct access to the child and the challenging behaviour. The challenging behaviour is recalled from memory with the possibility of faulty recollections. Parents might assume that a behaviour occurs more often than it actually occurs or that an important trigger is irrelevant. The net result can be inaccurate data ('information') regarding the antecedents and consequences of the challenging behaviour (O'Reilly *et al.*, 1994). Given these limitations, a behavioural interview should be followed up with direct observation of the challenging behaviour in the natural environment (the environment where it usually happens, e.g., at home).

Table 3.2: Suggestions for appropriate questions which may be included in a behavioural interview
(1) What is the challenging behaviour?
(2) Where does the behaviour take place?
(3) What time does the behaviour take place?
(4) How often does the behaviour occur?
(5) Who is present when the behaviour takes place?
(6) What occurred before (triggered) the behaviour?
(7) What occurred immediately after the behaviour?
(8) How did the child's mother respond?
(9) How did the child's father respond?
(10) How did sibling(s) respond?
(11) How did the others present respond?
(12) What reinforcer did the child access?
(13) What did the child avoid?

Direct observation

There are a number of direct observation instruments (e.g., ABC charts, scatterplots, behaviour record forms) which can be used to record data about challenging behaviour and its antecedents and consequences. A detailed description of each is beyond the scope of this chapter (for a detailed account see O'Reilly, 1997; Maurice, Green and Luce, 1996). The easiest and most frequently used observation instruments are variations of the ABC chart (see Figure 3.1). Such a chart may consist of space to record dates, times, and the ABC's of the challenging behaviour. The 'B' column is used to record a brief description of the challenging behaviour (e.g., Mark banged head against the wall). The 'A' column is used to record the antecedents of the challenging behaviour (e.g., Mark's mother asked him to put his toys away). The 'C' column is used to record the consequences of the challenging behaviour (e.g.,

Mark's mother stopped asking him to put his toys away). The child is typically observed over two to five days in the natural environment. It is not necessary to observe the child continuously throughout the day. A number of 30-minute observation sessions are usually adequate. Data from the behavioural interview may suggest when the challenging behaviour is likely to take place and this can be used to determine when and how often observations should occur.

Date	Time	Antecedent	Behaviour	Consequence
2.5.97	10 am	mother asked Mark to put toys away	Mark banged head against the wall	mother stopped asking him to put his toys away
2.5.97	11.15 am	mother asked Mark to put shoes on	Mark banged head against the cupboard	mother puts Mark's shoes on for him
2.5.97	12 noon	....	....	

Figure 3.1 An example of an ABC recording chart

A major advantage of observation in the natural environment is that it provides direct access to the child and the challenging behaviour. In addition, direct observation provides access to multiple variables and important data that may be missed in a behavioural interview (O'Neill, Horner, Albin, Storey and Sprague, 1990). Like most data-gathering techniques, direct observation in the natural setting has a number of disadvantages (see Lerman and Iwata, 1993). Perhaps, the most important of these are that direct observation can be time consuming and the practicalities of any given situation may not allow for it (e.g., parents may be involved in an activity which prevents them from immediately recording important information). Another disadvantage is that a child or anyone else in the child's environment may behave differently if they are aware that they are being observed. The result is that a change in a child's environment (i.e., in terms of the behaviour exhibited by the child or others) may mask, inhibit, or distort the natural environment to the extent that it may not reveal the function of the challenging behaviour. This is referred to as reactivity (Kazdin, 1980). A final disadvantage is that the data obtained from the behavioural interview and direct observation sessions is correlational. Correlational means that two or more things may have an association, but may not be causally related (i.e., one may not cause the other). For example, a parent asks the child to tidy her toys and the child starts a temper tantrum. The request is related in some way to the tantrum behaviour, but it is possible that something else is causing the tantrum (e.g., the presence of another sibling during the request). Without systematic or experimental manipulation of the environment, it is not possible to conclude definitively that the request is causally related to the behaviour (Lerman and Iwata, 1993).

Functional analysis

Functional analysis techniques have been used to assess and treat a variety of challenging behaviours including self-injury (Day, Rea, Schussler, Larsen and Johnson, 1988); stereotypy (Durand and Crimmins, 1988); and aggression (Slifer, Ivanic, Parrish, Page and Burgio, 1986). Functional analyses of behaviour constitute the final means of conducting an assessment of challenging behaviour. The most distinguishing feature of this method of analysis lies in its direct and systematic manipulation of antecedents and consequences that potentially occasion and maintain the behaviour. The systematic manipulation facilitates the confirmation of causal relationships between behaviour and its antecedents and consequences. The rationale behind conducting a functional analysis is very simple. If you think you have identified the correct antecedents and consequences for the behaviour, then you should be able to influence its occurrence by making sure that these antecedents or consequences are present. In other words, antecedents and consequences which are causally related to the behaviour (i.e., account for it) can be identified by recording changes in behaviour that occur when various antecedents and consequences are introduced to and removed from the individual (Lennox and Miltenberger, 1989). Unfortunately, the control necessary to conduct such an analysis is often difficult to obtain in the natural environment. What usually happens is that situations are specially arranged to allow for the analysis (i.e., analogue settings are designed which approximate the natural setting; see La Vigna and Donnellan, 1986). Once the conditions that control the behaviour are identified, these antecedents and consequences can then be manipulated in the natural environment.

There are a number of functional analysis procedures in which experimental control can be exercised. In all cases there should be at least one condition (experimental) in which the variable of interest (e.g., a parental request) is present and another condition (control) in which this variable is absent (Iwata et al., 1994). If you are trying to analyse the function of self-injurious behaviour (SIB), such as hand-biting, the following functional analysis might help. Consider a mother and child seated at a table working on a range of tasks that reflect those commonly used with the child, for example, putting objects into boxes or finding objects in a picture (e.g., using instructions such as 'Put in' and 'Where is?'). In **Condition 1** (no intervention) the mother gives instructions as normal and ignores any biting. The child's father observes the child for a certain length of time and records the number of biting episodes. In **Condition 2** (negative reinforcement) the mother gives instructions as normal but withdraws from the child for five seconds if the child engages in biting. When the five seconds are up she starts working with the child again. The child's father observes the child and records the number of biting episodes. In **Condition 3** (attention) the mother provides attention following any biting (e.g., 'Don't do that!'). The child's father observes the child and records the number of biting examples. By doing the above analysis you may find that data indicate that biting occurred most often in Condition 3 (i.e., when the mother provides attention) and least often in Condition 1 (when biting was ignored). These data suggest that ignoring biting behaviour would be the best form of intervention.

More complex functional analyses have been developed by Iwata, Dorsey, Slifer, Bauman, and Richman (1994) in which they compared several variables (i.e., possible reasons for the challenging behaviour) to determine the exact function of challenging behaviour. They used four conditions to assess the function of self-injurious behaviour (SIB) for nine individuals:

1. In **Condition 1** they wanted to find out if SIB occurred when attention was given as a consequence, in other words they set up a positive reinforcement condition. An adult was present in the room and remained three metres from the child. There were materials such as magazines and toys available, but no particular tasks or activities were provided. The adult delivered attention for self-injury or aggression but otherwise ignored the child. Attention consisted of verbal reprimands for approximately ten seconds.

2. In **Condition 2** they aimed to establish whether SIB occurred when escape from demands was permitted as a consequence, in other words they set up a negative reinforcement condition. A child was presented with difficult tasks. The tasks were presented continuously throughout the condition unless self-injury or aggression occurred. If SIB occurred, the task was removed for ten seconds or until the challenging behaviour stopped, at which point the task was immediately reinstated. The interactions between the child and adult were limited to prompts (i.e., no informal interactions occurred and no praise was given for correct responding).

3. In **Condition 3** they tried to establish whether engaging in SIB was reinforcing in itself, in other words, they set up an automatic

reinforcement condition. The child was in the therapy room alone, with no materials present, no access to either attention or toys.

4. **Condition 4** was used as a control condition. No attention was offered for SIB, no demands were made, play materials were available and attention was contingent on the absence of SIB (i.e., attention was given when no SIB occurred). This condition resembled the attention condition with the exception that the adult maintained a closer proximity and verbally interacted with the child every ten seconds regardless of behaviour.

Results of Iwata *et al.*'s study showed higher frequencies of SIB in a specific condition for six of the nine individuals. In other words, it was possible to identify the conditions in which the child engaged in SIB and those conditions in which s/he didn't. In technical terms we may say that the function of the problem behaviour for most of the children was identified. We will now look at an example in more detail.

case example

Bill is a six-year-old boy with the characteristics of autism. He exhibits a number of challenging behaviours including aggression and temper tantrums. Of particular concern to Bill's parents was his frequent screaming throughout the day. We will look at the different phases of assessment and intervention with Bill.

Phase 1 – Assessment

Behavioural interview

A semi-structured interview (based on the questions suggested above in Table 3.2) completed by Bill's mother and father indicated that screaming occurred intermittently throughout the day. The interview data also seemed to suggest that screaming was most likely to occur if Bill was asked to do something.

Direct observation

Following the behavioural interview, Bill's parents conducted direct observation sessions. Observation sessions were conducted three times per day (morning, afternoon and evening) with each session lasting for twenty minutes each. An ABC record sheet (see Figure 3.1) was used during each session to record the occurrence of the screaming behaviour, its antecedents and consequences.

Results of functional assessment and hypothesis development

Observational and interview data indicated that screaming occurred throughout the day but was more pronounced in the mornings and the evenings. In addition, screaming was most likely to occur if a request was made of Bill (e.g., 'Eat your dinner!'). Based on this data, we hypothesised (i.e., proposed) that Bill screamed to avoid following a request, suggesting that negative reinforcement was maintaining his challenging behaviour.

Functional analysis

To confirm this hypothesis, a functional analysis was conducted. A series of three conditions were used to examine the function of, or reason for, Bill's screaming. Each condition was assessed in five three-minute sessions. A brief description of each condition follows.

- **Condition 1: Attention:** Bill's mother remained approximately six feet away from him. Bill was allowed to play with books and toys. His mother delivered contingent attention[2] for screaming but otherwise ignored him (i.e., made no requests of Bill). Attention consisted of verbal reprimands.

- **Condition 2: Demand:** In this condition Bill was asked to perform a number of tasks (e.g., tidy toys or fold clothes). Requests to perform the tasks were presented continuously throughout the condition. If screaming occurred, the requests were stopped and Bill's mother moved away from him. When Bill calmed the requests were immediately reinstated.

- **Condition 3: Leisure:** This condition served as a control for the other conditions. The leisure condition was similar to the attention condition with the exception that Bill's mother remained in closer proximity and verbally interacted with Bill every ten seconds independent of behaviour displayed.

Results of functional analysis

Data indicated that Bill's screaming occurred most often in the demand condition (i.e., when his mother asked him to do something). We had hypothesised that the main reason (i.e., the primary function) of Bill's screaming behaviour was to avoid having to comply with a request. Through systematic manipulation of certain antecedents and consequences we had found this to be the case. We could now be much more confident in our diagnosis and develop a suitable intervention.

---

2   The attention was 'contingent' in the sense that it only occurred if screaming occurred.

Phase 2 – Intervention

Based on the data obtained from the functional assessment and analysis, we decided that a suitable intervention would have to involve adjustment of the way requests were made of Bill (Taylor et al., 1996). Bill's parents were instructed to stop making requests in the presence of screaming. When Bill calmed he was taught a more acceptable way to indicate his reluctance to comply (e.g., shake head and say 'No!'). This was done by modelling (i.e., Bill's parents demonstrated appropriate behaviour while he observed) and verbal instruction. If the request was something with which Bill needed to comply, the following strategies were used as appropriate (see Taylor et al., 1996):

(1) choice (i.e., Bill was provided with a choice of alternatives)

(2) pacing (i.e., Bill's parents described specifically each step of the behaviour and indicated the possible reinforcers that were available)

(3) pre-task requesting (i.e., before making a request that was unlikely to be followed, Bill's parents made two or three requests that Bill was likely to comply with before making the request with which he was less likely to comply).

Alternative interventions for Bill

We had found the main function of Bill's screaming behaviour. If, however, the functional assessment and functional analysis had indicated that the function(s) of Bill's screaming were: (1) attention seeking, (2) seeking access to reinforcers, or (3) physical stimulation, we would have used different kinds of interventions. For example we might have used one of the following interventions:

(1) if Bill's screaming had had the function of achieving attention we would have advised Bill's parents to ignore the screaming, maybe even to leave the room in order to ensure that Bill did not receive any attention for screaming behaviour.

(2) if Bill's screaming had had the function of gaining him access to a reinforcer we would have advised Bill's parents to deny him access to the desired object. When he has settled, they would be advised to explain to him that he can't have the desired object until he stops screaming and asks for it properly (e.g., holds out his hand and says 'Please').

(3) if Bill's screaming had had the function of gaining physical stimulation Bill's parents would be advised to reinforce low rates of screaming each hour (i.e., set a criterion of only three screaming outbursts each hour). If Bill met this criteria, his parents would provide reinforcement and explain to him why he was being

rewarded. In addition, Bill's parents might attempt to continually engage him in appropriate behaviour by providing lots of stimulating activities.

Conclusion

Challenging behaviour can be a major concern for parents of children with autism. Often these behaviours are resistant to conventional methods of child rearing practice and children with autism who are exhibiting challenging behaviour may be exposed to unnecessarily aversive and restrictive procedures (e.g., time-out and other forms of punishment). The use of aversive punishment procedure is generally avoided by today's behaviour analysts, especially because such methods may compound the problem by eliciting additional disruptive behaviour such as temper tantrums or escape-avoidance behaviour (Luce and Dyer, 1996) and invariably leading to greater isolation for the child. The kinds of functional assessment and functional analysis techniques reported in this chapter allow for a much more positive approach. They lead to interventions that are uniquely matched to the particular function of the behaviour and are therefore much more likely to lead to effective behavioural change (O'Neill, *et al.*, 1990).

You may find that doing a functional assessment and analysis seems like a complicated business. We agree that this kind of work may not be for the parent who is trying to come to terms with the immense wealth of new knowledge that they have to acquire in order to carry out even quite basic behaviour analytic programmes of intervention. For a proper and full functional analysis you may well have to rely on your behaviour analyst. However, we feel that it is important to introduce you to the depth of analysis required to achieve change with some of the more difficult behaviours that you may encounter with your child. The important message from this chapter for you may be that Behaviour Analysis has developed methods and techniques to deal with the most difficult behaviours, even if it takes quite a bit of training to be able to carry these out.

References

Carr, E.G. and Durand, V.M. (1985) Reducing behavior problems through functional communication training. *Journal of Applied Behavior Analysis, 18,* 111–126.

Day, R.M., Rea, J.A., Schussler, N.G., Larsen, S.E. and Johnson, W.L. (1988) A functionally based approach to the treatment of self-injurious behavior. *Behavior Modification, 12,* 565–589.

Durand, V.M. and Carr, E.G. (1987) Social influences on 'self-stimulatory' behavior: Analysis and treatment application. *Journal of Applied Behavior Analysis, 20,* 119–132.

Durand, V.M. and Crimmins, D.B. (1988) Identifying the variables maintaining self-injurious behavior. *Journal of Autism and Developmental Disorders, 18,* 99–117.

Gaylord-Ross, R., Haring, T.G., Breen, C. and Pitts-Conway, V. (1984) The training and generalization of social interaction skills with autistic youth. *Journal of Applied Behavior Analysis, 17*, 229–247.

Haring, T.G., Kennedy, C.H., Adams, M.J. and Pitts-Conway, V. (1987) Teaching generalization of purchasing skills across community settings to autistic youth using videotape modeling. *Journal of Applied Behavior Analysis, 20*, 89–96.

Iwata, B.A., Dorsey, M.E., Slifer, K.J., Bauman, K.E. and Richman, G.S. (1994) Toward a functional analysis of self-injury. *Journal of Applied Behavior Analysis, 27*, 197–209. Reprinted from *Analysis and Intervention in Developmental Disabilities* (1982) 2, 3–20.

Kazdin, A.E. (1980) *Behavior Modification in Applied Settings*. Homewood, Illinois: Dorsey.

Kennedy, C.H. and Souza, G. (1995) Functional analysis and treatment of eye poking. *Journal of Applied Behavior Analysis, 28*, 27–37.

La Vigna, G.D. and Donnellan, A. (1986) *Alternatives to Punishment: Solving Behavior Problems with Non-Aversive Strategies*. New York: Irvington.

Lennox, D.B. and Miltenberger, R.G. (1989) Conducting a functional assessment of problem behavior in applied settings. *Journal of the Association for Persons with Severe Handicaps, 14*, 304–311.

Lerman, D.C. and Iwata, B.A. (1993) Descriptive and experimental analyses of variables maintaining self-injurious behavior. *Journal of Applied Behavior Analysis, 26*, 293–319.

Lovaas, O.I. (1987) Behavioral treatment and normal educational and intellectual functioning in young autistic children. *Journal of Consulting and Clinical Psychology, 55*, 3–9.

Lovaas, O.I. and Favel, J.E. (1987) Protection for clients undergoing aversive/restrictive interventions. *Education and Treatment of Children, 10*, 311–325.

Lovaas, O.I. and Smith, T. (1988) Intensive behavioral treatment for young autistic children. In B.B. Lahey and A.E. Kazdin (eds) *Advances in Clinical Child Psychology, 11*, 285–324. New York: Plenum.

Lovaas, O.I. and Smith, T. (1989) A comprehensive behavioral theory of autistic children: Paradigm for research and treatment. *Journal of Behavior Therapy and Experimental Psychiatry, 20*, 17–29.

Luce, S.C. and Dyer, (1996) Answers to commonly asked questions. In C. Maurice, G. Green and S.C. Luce (eds) *Behavioral Intervention for Young Children with Autism: A Manual for Parents and Professionals* (pp. 345–357) Texas: Pro-Ed.

Maurice, C., Green, G. and Luce, S.C. (eds) (1996) *Behavioral Intervention for Young Children with Autism: A Manual for Parents and Professionals*. Texas: Pro-Ed.

O'Neill, R.E., Horner, R.H., Albin, R., Storey, K. and Sprague, J. (1990) *Functional Analysis: A Practical Assessment Guide*. Sycamore IL: Sycamore Press.

O'Reilly, M.F. (1997) Assessing challenging behaviour of persons with severe mental disabilities. In K. Dillenburger, M.F. O'Reilly, and M. Keenan (eds) *Advances in Behaviour Analysis*. Dublin, University College Dublin Press.

O'Reilly, M.F., O'Kane, N.P. and Taylor, I. (1994) Current trends in behavioural assessment of problem behaviour. *Thornfield Journal, 17*, 18–23.

Repp, A.C. and Singh, N.N. (1990) *Perspectives on the Use of Nonaversive and Aversive Interventions for Persons with Developmental Disabilities*. Sycamore, Illinois: Sycamore Publishing.

Repp, A.C., Singh, N.N., Olinger, E. and Olson, D.R. (1990) The use of functional analysis to test causes of self-injurious behavior: Rationale, current status, and future directions. *Journal of Mental Deficiency Research, 34*, 95–105.

Skinner, B.F. (1957) *Verbal Behavior.* New York: Appleton–Century–Croft.

Skinner, B.F. (1982) Contrived reinforcement. *The Behavior Analyst, 5*, 3–8.

Slifer, K.J., Ivanic, M.T., Parrish. J.M., Page. T.J. and Burgio, L.D. (1986) Assessment and treatment of multiple behavior problems exhibited by a profoundly retarded adolescent. *Journal of Behavior Therapy and Experimental Psychiatry, 17*, 203–213.

Taylor, I., O'Reilly, M.F. and Lancioni, G. (1996) A consultation model to train teachers to treat challenging behaviour. *International Journal of Disability, Development and Education, 43*, 203–218.

Whitman, T.L. (1990) Self-regulation and mental retardation. *American Journal of Mental Retardation, 94*, 347–362.

CHAPTER 4

Colin's Story

Laura McKay, Mickey Keenan and Karola Dillenburger

In this chapter we describe the first year of treatment for Colin in some detail.[1] We have decided to outline the procedures used for each of the target behaviours in the sequence in which they occurred. We felt that this sequential description would give you a full picture of the amount of work necessary to apply Behaviour Analysis properly with your child. As well as reporting the results we discuss pertinent issues relevant to each intervention. Finally, at the end of the chapter you will find a full discussion of the most important points that arose throughout the year. This is the longest chapter in the book and we have included a guide at the bottom of the pages describing the interventions to help you keep track of their sequential order. The interventions are numbered from 1 to 17 and above each number is a box. As each intervention is described the appropriate box is filled in.

Colin's early years

Up until Colin's first birthday there was nothing that suggested that he would have any problems. He was the youngest of five children, born after a normal pregnancy and a straightforward delivery. He weighed 7lb 5oz and became a contented and alert baby. He was making 'mama' and 'dada' sounds by 12 months and was able to walk around holding onto furniture. Although his parents did not notice any significant episode, by the time Colin was 20 months it had become obvious that something was different about him. At his belated 18 months assessment the health visitor expressed a number of concerns. Colin was small and light for his age, with a very immature appearance; he could have easily been taken for a child six months younger.

---

1   All names have been changed to preserve privacy.

He did not respond to the hearing tests and it was difficult to physically keep him in the room for the assessment. The health visitor made reference to hearing loss, possible brain damage, and developmental delay.

Between the ages of 20 months and 3 years and 9 months Colin was seen by dozens of health professionals, including several community medical officers, audiologists, ear, nose, and throat (ENT) specialists, speech therapists, psychologists, paediatricians, an occupational therapist, a physiotherapist, and several health visitors (see Table 4.1). Colin was becoming more and more resistant to change, his language was limited to very basic demands and labels, and family life was severely disrupted because it was too much of a battle to take him visiting or shopping. He had been assessed as having moderate learning difficulties and professionals were beginning to talk about special schools and units. They were talking about the possibility that he was on the autistic spectrum and the need for a Statement of Special Educational Needs was being considered. Shortly after this, the consultant psychiatrist diagnosed Colin as having Asperger's Syndrome and Attention Deficit/Hyperactivity Disorder. He was extremely active, and if restrained (e.g., holding his hand, carrying him, or using a child harness) he became extremely upset and it became a thoroughly aversive situation for the whole family. He depended on routines, for example, he became upset if his mother, Laura, varied the route to the nursery school, even if she parked the car in a different place. In nursery school he refused to join in story time or planned activities, preferring solitary repetitive play with toy cars, water, and sand. However, he adjusted quickly to routines such as those used for going to school, having a break at school, or going home. At home he was seldom still and the parents had to lock windows and internal doors. He did not respond to his name, he slept little, waking frequently and was very difficult to settle in bed again. He did not do what he was told and everything seemed a struggle. Despite this litany of negative characteristics there was a positive side to him, he was a good-natured child and he could count very well.

Table 4.1: Assessment by professionals

Colin's age at assessment

1 year 8 months	Colin was referred to speech and language therapy by a health visitor.
2 years	Colin was assessed by a speech and language therapist as having severely disordered communication development. Both comprehension and expression were severely affected.

Self-distracting behaviour and echolalia were present.

2 years 2 months Colin was referred to psychology service by a clinical medical officer.

2 years 6 months Colin began speech and language therapy. A supportive programme was implemented with some interruptions due to staff shortage.

3 years Colin was seen at a developmental clinic but '...his pronounced attention deficit prevented any formal assessment taking place' (educational psychologist report). The only help offered to Colin's parents at this point was the advice to deal with any problem behaviours in a consistent manner.

3 years 2 months Colin was seen at home in the presence of his father and mother. Educational psychologist report: 'Again a formal assessment using individual tests was not appropriate because of [Colin's] unwillingness to settle. The principal area of concern was [Colin's] poor level of attention, control, and listening. This lack of attentiveness hindered his expressive vocabulary development.'

Continued attendance at the local play group was encouraged because it was felt that interaction with his peers would aid the acquisition of communication skills. Colin received speech therapy and tuition from the pre-school services aimed at extending his on-task time for table-top activities. However, initially teacher visits were unproductive because Colin engaged in lone and reclusive activities.

3 years 2 months Clinical medical officer report: 'He has general developmental delay which is most marked in the area of speech and language development. [Colin] has a very short concentration span.[He] tends to play on his own and does not mix well with other children. [Colin] feels more secure when things happen according to fixed routines.'

Educational services noted a greater acceptance of the pre-school teacher and a growth in fine motor skills. Colin was imitating some simple words and was able to name some basic objects but he did this inconsistently. He could count to 20 and identify number symbols up to 10. When interested he remained on task for up to 15 minutes. Interaction time and quality were on his terms as he resisted direction.

Report from pre-school home teacher: '[Colin] can feed himself and drink from a cup. He can take off and put on his shoes and other articles of clothing, though needs assistance with fastenings. Most of his language is to convey needs, e.g., drink, biscuit. Most of his phrases involve echolalia … Generally any interaction with [Colin] is on his own terms.'

3 years 3 months   Health visitor report: '[Colin's] nursing needs are only related to his toileting needs. Needs to be taken to the bathroom frequently.'

3 years 4 months   Pre-school home teacher notes greater willingness and interest in naming. Educational psychologist report: 'His awareness of toileting behaviour had improved.'

Clinical medical officer report: '[Colin's] physical health is good. Various investigations were carried out to see if there was any medical basis for [Colin's] difficulties, but these were all normal.'

3 years 8 months   Although Colin's expressive and receptive language had improved somewhat, there was still '…a good deal of echolalia and repetitive expression. There was no functional interaction with peers' (Educational psychologist report).

3 years 9 months   Colin was observed at play group. This observation revealed less hyperactivity, but the lone play and drifting from one activity to another continued.

3 years 9 months   Four class-room observations highlighted a very pronounced lack of social awareness. Educational psychologist report: '[Colin] pays scant regard or ignores group and class activities. He often wanders about the class room oblivious to the main class activity. While peers in close proximity are reacting off each other [Colin] remains egocentrically preoccupied with the toy cars, having no urge to engage socially.'

3 years 10 months Colin was assessed using the CARS Scale. Educational psychologist report: 'The results specifically indicated a language delay, social aloofness, some degree of obsessiveness, poor adaptation to change, high level of activity and low level of attention control.' At this time it was agreed that a Statement of Special Educational Needs should be initiated.

Events leading up to Behaviour Analysis with Colin

By the time Colin was three years and ten months he had received intermittent speech and language therapy and he had been given tuition from the pre-school services for one hour per week for some months. He also attended the local play group. He had received no therapy specifically aimed at reducing any of the other problems that the numerous assessments had identified. The general approach by health professionals to Colin can be summarised by such statements as 'he should be encouraged and given opportunities to develop'. No detailed plans of how this could be achieved were given to his parents.

Finally, a Statement of Special Educational Needs was prepared for Colin in which his difficulties were identified as follows:

(1) Emotional and behavioural difficulties;

(2) Severe communication disorder;

(3) Short level of concentration, easily distracted;

(4) Difficulties in establishing and maintaining balanced relationships with adults and peers.

The general opinion of health professionals was that school provision should be facilitated in a special needs class. Colin's parents were distraught. This was not the schooling of their choice. Again Laura went to her general practitioner (GP) for advice and support. The GP had previously given her advice and reading material (e.g., Pryor, 1984), which had helped Laura to toilet-train Colin when he was three-and-a-half years old. At the time Laura had thought that Colin could not be toilet trained and she was very pleased with the effectiveness of the method recommended by her GP. She was hoping that he could help again. The GP recommended that the parents speak with a behaviour analyst at the University of Ulster at Coleraine,

Psychology Department who was a friend of the GP. The behaviour analyst agreed to work on a voluntary basis with Colin and his parents. A training programme was set up with the aim of educating Colin's parents to become his therapists.

Training parents in Behaviour Analysis

In the main, the parent training programme in Applied Behaviour Analysis (ABA) was carried out with Colin's mother, Laura. Training initially took place on a weekly basis in the behaviour analyst's home with Colin present; occasionally a second behaviour analyst was available. Later this training was phased out to fortnightly sessions, and, later again, monthly sessions were offered. Finally, after about one year, training sessions were terminated and follow-up sessions were offered at Laura's request. The details presented in the following pages bear witness to some of the work undertaken during this year.

Training concentrated on introducing Laura to the basics of Behaviour Analysis (Keenan and Dillenburger, in press). This included the identification of target behaviours (as described in Chapter 1), functional assessment of the target behaviours (as described in Chapter 3), and the design of treatment procedures and data-based decision making (as described in this chapter). Laura gathered data throughout the week and presented this to the behaviour analyst for discussion and informed decision making on each visit. Observations of Colin during each visit were used to verify the progress made by Laura. On this basis further treatment plans progressed.

Usually during a training session Colin was given a range of toys to allow him to engage in free play. His behaviour was observed and used to illustrate the issues that needed to be addressed at the time. For example, when positive reinforcement was discussed the second behaviour analyst who was playing with Colin discovered that a certain toy truck functioned as a reinforcer for aspects of Colin's play behaviour. This finding was used to illustrate to Laura the power of positive reinforcement and the importance of a functional definition of reinforcement. In summary, Laura was taught a basic course in Behaviour Analysis and guided in how to change Colin's behaviours.

Setting

Most of the treatment took place in Colin's home. His home is situated in a rural area in Northern Ireland. Colin lives there with both parents, his three older sisters and one older brother. Most of the treatment took place in the utility room of the home. Colin was usually seated at a table. Distractions such as television and visitors were kept to a minimum. Generalisation training took place in other rooms of the home, such as the kitchen and

Colin's bedroom. Usually Laura was seated opposite Colin. For most of the work Laura was the main therapist, for generalisation training Colin's father, sisters and friends participated.

Behavioural assessment

One of the first tasks given to Laura during the initial assessment was to compile a list of behavioural problems that she had observed in Colin. This was done to help strike a balance between her blindly following the instructions of the behaviour analyst and finding a way to give her confidence in overcoming behaviours that she had considered intractable. It was going to be a long haul and her work needed to be reinforced by early successes if she was going to stay the pace.

Laura found that the following behaviours needed intervention:

(1) Colin seemed unable to pick up cues from the external environment, for example, his eye contact was poor, fleeting, or non-existent. He had poor use of language, poor use of gesture, and lack of social skills. He spoke in two-word sentences and responded to questions with echolalia (i.e., he repeated the question rather than answer it). He was unable to initiate or sustain a conversation with familiar adults and children, especially with those he rarely saw (e.g., consultants). He never asked questions like 'What is that?'

(2) Colin was not distractible when focused on one activity, e.g., if he was walking from one room to the next and there were objects on the floor, he walked over these objects instead of around them; when there were people in his way he pushed past them rather then walking around them; if he was doing something, such as playing with a particular toy, he did not leave the toy, even if Laura offered him another toy or something to eat or drink.

(3) Colin was fixed on routines, e.g., he expected exactly the same utensils or cutlery at every meal, and he became upset if his pattern of activity was interrupted. If an activity was first carried out in a certain way, he expected it to be repeated exactly the same the next time, even if it was not appropriate to the occasion. He tidied up cupboards in speech therapy, for example, and demanded that the GP's computer was set in a certain way. Colin also was reluctant to take up a task if he had initially rejected it (e.g., if he had refused to paint he would not do so later).

(4) Colin lost interest in a toy or object once it was removed, e.g., if he was playing with a toy and someone took it away from him, he did not try to get it back. Although Colin seemed to lose interest in most things once they were removed, this was not always the case. There were certain objects, such as toy cars or tractors, for which he showed much more

prolonged interest. At times, when he had lost interest in a toy and someone else had begun to play with this toy, he showed renewed interest. For example, he played with a toy purse and did not pursue it when it was removed; however, he showed renewed interest if someone opened and closed the purse, or made it 'interesting' in some other way.

This list provided a useful starting point. It helped us to identify some of the target behaviours that we needed to work on. The identification of target behaviours was, however, by no means a straightforward or pre-determined process. We used a variety of methods to find out what behaviours we should teach Colin at what time; we used our observations of Colin's behaviour during parent training sessions; we used Laura's knowledge of his typically developing older siblings; we asked Colin's nursery school teacher for a list of the behaviours that distinguished Colin from his peers; we used the report from the educational psychologist to identify behaviours that would need to be in place if Colin was to be placed in mainstream education.

The process of identifying target behaviours evolved throughout the year. ABA became part of daily life. In this chapter we describe 17 of the many interventions that we used. Table 4.2 lists the target behaviours sequentially.

Applied Behaviour Analysis with Colin

1. Target behaviour

Behavioural treatment began when Colin was aged three years and ten months. The first behaviour that was targeted for change was his eye contact. Laura had observed that Colin did not seek or hold eye contact when someone was talking to him or when he wanted something. Since eye contact is one of the most fundamental of social skills and is essential for receiving instructions and learning from others, including his mother, it was selected as the first target behaviour. A clear definition as to what Laura was trying to achieve was necessary. The initial definition of the target behaviour that was agreed upon was this: eye contact was considered to have occurred if Colin offered a direct glance or stare into another person's eyes. A random gaze was not considered appropriate even if it included brief contact with the other's eyes. This definition seemed to be appropriate, but there were complications. Colin did not even look up when his name was called. It was decided, then, that this behavioural deficit would be the first one to be addressed.

1   2   3   4   5   6   7   8   9   10 11 12 13 14 15 16 17

Table 4.2: Target behaviours		
Intervention	**Date**	**Target behviour**
Intervention 1	2–11 Dec 1995	Eye contact (latency)
Intervention 2	29 Dec 1995	Self help skills (stereotypic behaviour)
Intervention 3	1–5 Jan 1996	Play skills (flexibility)
Intervention 4	1–4 Feb 1996	Verbal behaviour (expressive language)
Intervention 5	3–6 March 1996	Verbal behaviour (echolalia, frequency)
Intervention 6	3 March 1996	Eye contact (generalisation)
Intervention 7	6–19 March 1996	Verbal behaviour (fluency of speech)
Intervention 8	March 1996	Object permanence (pursue hidden toy)
Intervention 9	16 March – 4 July 1996	Verbal behaviour (echolalia)
Intervention 10	14 May – 3 June 1996	Communication (jigsaw puzzles)
Intervention 11	29 May – 4 June 1996	Eye contact (during intense play)
Intervention 12	8.–27 June 1996	Eye contact (the 'looking game')
Intervention 13	23 June – 10 July 1996	Eye contact (duration)
Intervention 14	17 Aug – 15 Sept 1996	Play skills (relaxation)
Intervention 15	17 Aug – 17 Sept 1996	Play skills (peer play)
Intervention 16	20 Aug – 4 Sept 1996	Play skills (role play)
Intervention 17	1–26 Oct 1996	Academic tasks (table top activities)

The technical term for the time it takes between the onset of a stimulus (e.g., calling his name) and the occurrence of a behaviour (e.g., eye contact) is 'latency'. The first target, therefore, was a decrease in the latency with which Colin made eye contact after he was instructed to do so, that is, after a verbal prompt. Initially the verbal prompts chosen were the words 'Colin, look at me' or 'look at me'. Later in treatment (second procedure) this was simplified to the verbal prompt 'Colin' when Laura wanted him to look at her. At this point it did not matter how long Colin looked at Laura, it was important only that he did look up.

1 2 3 4 5 6 7 8 9 10 11 12 13 14 15 16 17

FIRST PROCEDURE

For this intervention Colin was seated at a table and told to play with a relatively difficult jigsaw puzzle and a pack of snap cards depicting television characters with which Colin was familiar (TV Tots). Some of his sisters were also present. While Colin played with the other children or built card houses on his own, Laura gave the direct prompt to look at her and then timed his response with the aid of a timer and noted the results on a note pad.

During the first 20 times, or trials as they are called, Laura did nothing else other than prompt Colin to look at her. The data she collected during these trials constituted the 'baseline'. Taking a baseline offered Laura the opportunity to get a clearer picture of the behaviour she was going to change. It also provided a yardstick with which to measure the success of her intervention; if the intervention was not successful, data collected during the baseline and during the intervention would look fairly similar. Baseline taking was followed by a brief break during which Colin was allowed to leave the table.

Eye contact

■ □ □ □ □ □ □ □ □ □ □ □ □ □ □ □ □

1 2 3 4 5 6 7 8 9 10 11 12 13 14 15 16 17

When Colin was brought back to the table at the end of his break he was asked to continue his play with the jigsaw puzzle and the TV Tots snap cards. Again he was prompted to establish eye contact with the words 'Colin, look at me' or 'look at me'. This time reinforcement was delivered immediately after eye contact was made. Edible reinforcers such as Smarties® or white chocolate buttons as well as social reinforcers like hugs and verbal praise were given immediately after he engaged in the agreed-upon behaviour. The initial intervention was carried out for 18 trials. The intervention was repeated in the kitchen three days later for eight trials.

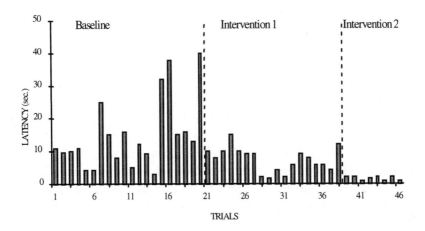

Figure 4.1 The latency with which Colin made eye contact with his mother following the prompt 'Colin, look at me' or 'Look at me'

RESULTS

Figure 4.1 presents the results achieved during the first intervention. The latency with which Colin made eye contact following the direct prompt from Laura to look at her was the dependant measure. During baseline an average latency of 14 seconds was measured. A decrease in latency was observed during the first intervention sequence. Latency during this sequence averaged

6.5 seconds. During the second intervention sequence three days later, latency reduced to an average of 1.5 seconds.

DISCUSSION

The results of the first intervention show a dramatic reduction in the latency with which Colin responded appropriately by making eye contact following the direct prompt to look at Laura. Given that eye contact is one of the most basic components of social interaction it was important to establish this behaviour before further intervention could be considered.

During the intervention a number of problems were observed by Laura. First, during baseline taking there were a lot of distractions for Colin from the other children, the computer made a lot of noise and others were coming and going in and out of the treatment room. However, Laura observed that Colin was sitting for a considerable time without any serious attempts to leave the table or to become uncooperative. This observation was important for Laura. It showed her that Colin could learn new behaviours and she was therefore motivated to continue the treatment.

Another important point was that during the first intervention Laura observed that edible reinforcers such as Smarties® quickly ceased to be effective. However, she discovered that hugs and praise increasingly functioned as reinforcers. The intervention was terminated after 18 trials because Colin was becoming uncooperative, having sat for an unusually long time. Three days later the intervention was repeated in the kitchen. This time Colin was on his own. As soon as he saw the timer he said 'Mickey', the name of the behaviour analyst. On this occasion timing Colin's response was difficult because it was too rapid. He also had begun to demand chocolate when he responded and tried to search Laura's sleeves for sweets. Laura considered that if she gave Colin chocolates when he became demanding, this kind of inappropriate behaviour would probably be reinforced. Instead, Laura decided to terminate the intervention.

During this intervention Laura had used the direct prompt 'Colin, look at me' or 'look at me'. The reason for this was that during the first training session with Laura she called 'Colin' many times without any response from him. It had soon become obvious that calling his name had no control over his behaviour. Laura was, therefore, instructed to avoid calling Colin's name repeatedly throughout the day and use the direct instruction 'look at me'. However, it is not usual in daily life to give this kind of direct instruction to achieve eye contact. Usually one's name functions as a stimulus for eye

contact. Laura therefore wanted to establish the term 'Colin' as a stimulus for Colin to make eye contact. Equally, most people make eye contact when they hear their name regardless of the identity of the caller or their location. Colin therefore had to learn not only to make eye contact when his name was called but also to generalise this behaviour to other people and to other situations.

SECOND PROCEDURE

Again Colin was seated at a table in the utility room, this time with his sister Ruth. They were playing with two new jigsaw puzzles. Laura called out 'Colin' and timed the latency with which Colin made eye contact. After a brief baseline she reinforced eye contact with edible, social, and arbitrary reinforcers (stickers).

The next goal was to ensure that Colin made eye contact not only in the utility room. Generalisation training was carried out in different rooms, first in the kitchen, then in Colin's bedroom. In the kitchen Colin played on the floor with his usual toys and occasionally other children walked in and joined his play. Laura called 'Colin' to initiate eye contact. In his bedroom, Colin and his sister Ruth were playing with a floor puzzle during the intervention.

In order to ensure that generalisation of the target behaviour was not only happening in other situations but also with other people, the procedure was repeated by another person, Colin's father, Geoffrey. He worked with Colin in the utility room for two sessions and in the kitchen for the third session. Colin was seated at the table with a jumble of jigsaw pieces and Geoffrey called 'Colin' to initiate eye contact. Baseline taking and intervention were the same as during the earlier intervention. During intervention edible and social reinforcers were given immediately each time Colin made eye contact.

RESULTS

Figures 4.2 to 4.6 show the results of the intervention and generalisation trials.

When working with Laura in the utility room the baseline latency averaged 12.4 seconds. During intervention the average latency was 6.1 seconds. When working with her in the kitchen the baseline latency averaged 5 seconds; during intervention the average latency was 1.6 seconds.

When working with her in his own bedroom the baseline latency averaged 9 seconds, and during the intervention the average was 8.2 seconds.

Colin worked on two occasions with his father in the utility room (see Figure 4.5).

■ ☐ ☐ ☐ ☐ ☐ ☐ ☐ ☐ ☐ ☐ ☐ ☐ ☐ ☐ ☐ ☐

1 2 3 4 5 6 7 8 9 10 11 12 13 14 15 16 17

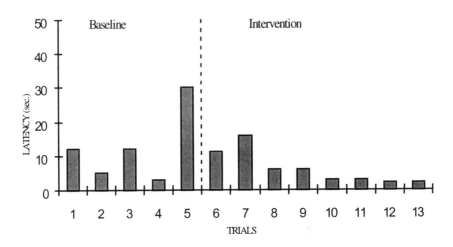

Figure 4.2 The latency with which Colin made eye contact with his mother following the prompt 'Colin' when both of them were in the utility room

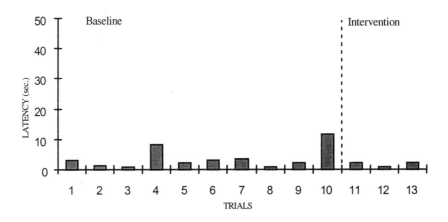

Figure 4.3 The latency with which Colin made eye contact with his mother following the prompt 'Colin' when both of them were in the kitchen

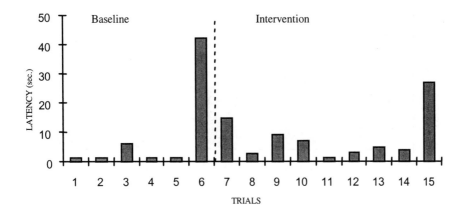

Figure 4.4 The latency with which Colin made eye contact with his mother following the prompt 'Colin' when both of them were in Colin's bedroom

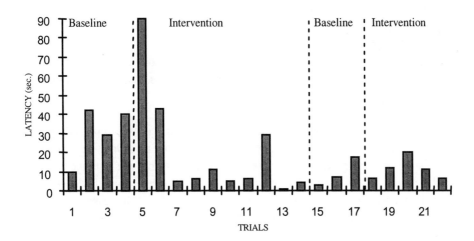

Figure 4.5 The latency with which Colin made eye contact with his father following the prompt 'Colin' when both of them were in the utility room

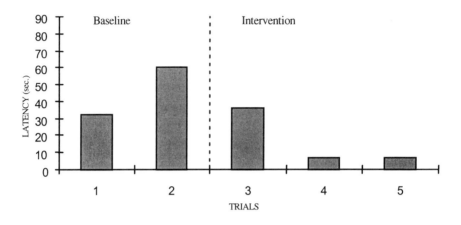

Figure 4.6 The latency with which Colin made eye contact with his father following the prompt 'Colin' when both of them were in the kitchen

On the first occasion the baseline latency averaged 30.2 seconds, and during intervention this decreased to 20 seconds. During the second, baseline latency averaged 9 seconds, but during the intervention a slight increase to 11 seconds was observed.

When Colin worked with his father in the kitchen the baseline latency averaged 46 seconds, and during intervention this decreased to 16.6 seconds.

DISCUSSION

During this procedure the direct instruction 'look at me' was replaced by Colin's own name. When Laura called 'Colin', baseline measures indicated that the latency with which Colin responded by making eye contact was similar to the baseline during the trials when the direct prompt had been used. However, the latency during the intervention soon decreased. This decrease generalised across settings and people. There was one exception. This exception occurred when his father was working with him for the second time in the utility room; a small increase in latency was observed.

Laura noted a number of important points in the delivery of reinforcers. First, she was using edible reinforcers, such as chocolates, during the early

trials. After a few trials Colin started to say 'chocolate' and held his hand out for chocolate after he had made very brief eye contact. Laura did not give him chocolate at this point. Colin ran towards Laura and gave her a hug, thus finishing the trial. Chocolate had lost its function as a reinforcer and Laura had to find an alternative. She gave Colin stickers and continued the trials. Colin continued working well and the latency of eye contact continued to decrease. However, Colin 'demanded' chocolate again when his father was working with him and his father gave him chocolate. Geoffrey observed that 'Colin became restless and it was difficult to get him to stay with the activity'. He eventually gave up because he found Colin 'too easily distracted'.

Colin's response to edible reinforcers was interesting for a number of reasons. If Laura had given him the chocolate following his demands, instead of switching to using stickers as reinforcers, she might have accidentally reinforced demanding behaviour rather than eye contact. This can happen and is precisely what happened with Colin's father. He accidentally reinforced Colin's inappropriate behaviour and consequently found it difficult to keep Colin on task. Another thing that sometimes happens is that a child may start to demand a treat before making eye contact. If you give your child the treat that you were planning to use as a reinforcer before s/he has made eye contact, s/he might then refuse to make eye contact. Again this can happen very easily but it more closely resembles bribery than reinforcement. People sometimes confuse bribery with reinforcement. There are, however, clear and important differences between them. To bribe is to 'promise, offer, or give something, usually money, to (a person) to produce services or gain influence, esp. illegally' (*Collins English Dictionary*, 1991). That is, something is given *before* the behaviour occurs. The term reinforcement has been defined in Chapter 1 as a term that refers to an outcome after a *consequence* has been delivered. This outcome determines how we describe the function of a stimulus, i.e., whether or not it has reinforcing qualities.

2. Target behaviour

The next intervention took place when Colin was aged three years and eleven months. Laura had identified that Colin only used one particular old yellow plastic cup when he wanted a drink. It was stained and rough, but he refused to drink from anything else. Laura had seen this kind of fixation on routines in a number of areas and the drinking cup seemed to be a good starting point for teaching her how to design an intervention.

■ ■ □ □ □ □ □ □ □ □ □ □ □ □ □ □ □

1 2 3 4 5 6 7 8 9 10 11 12 13 14 15 16 17

Colin was seated at a table. Three different cups were placed in front of him, including his favourite old yellow cup. Different drinks were put into each of these three different cups. The old yellow cup was always filled with water, while a blue cup was filled either with blackberry juice or Diet Pepsi®, and a cup with a picture of a leaf on it was filled either with orange juice, milk, blackberry juice or Diet Pepsi®. Colin was invited to sip from all three cups and put them back on the table. He was then invited to sip them all again and choose one.

RESULTS

Table 4.3 shows the results obtained during four trials.

Table 4.3: Eliminating stereotypic behaviour		
No. of trial	**Yellow cup**	**Blue cup**	**'Leaf' cup**
1.	Water	Blackberry juice	Orange juice X
2.	Water	Blackberry juice	Milk X
3.	Water	Diet Pepsi X	Blackberry juice
4.	Water	Blackberry juice	Diet Pepsi X

For each trial Colin sipped all three cups and the 'x' indicates which cup he chose. During the final trial he just looked at the three cups and said 'leaf cup' and took it. Later that day Laura found Colin in poor form and he asked for his yellow cup. Laura gave it to him filled with water. Colin poured out the water and replaced it with the juice from the blue cup. Laura refilled the yellow cup with water and the blue cup with juice and Colin chose the blue cup. He has since been happily using the blue or 'leaf cup' and will go and fill them for himself.

1 2 3 4 5 6 7 8 9 10 11 12 13 14 15 16 17

DISCUSSION

Within four trials Colin's persistent behaviour of drinking only from one particular cup was changed. This change generalised to other situations and Colin now drinks from a variety of drinking cups. For professionals this isn't a dramatic finding, but for a parent the sense of empowerment at such a simple change in behaviour can be quite profound. In addition, the success in changing this long-standing behaviour had a number of side effects. First, it helped Colin to draw less attention to himself in public situations. Second, it increased Laura's confidence that she would be able to achieve long lasting change with Colin. Third, this intervention helped identify potential reinforcers for Colin that might be used during other procedures.

3. Target behaviour

This intervention took place when Colin was four years old. The nursery school teacher had commented that Colin played alone or alongside others and did not engage in conversation with children. She wrote in her contribution to the Statement for Special Educational Needs:

> 'He finds it difficult to communicate, except on his own terms and his language is poor for a four-year-old. He speaks to himself when he plays, e.g., 'crash, crash digger' and 'put on wheels.' Sometimes he becomes upset when other children want to come and join him on the mat (especially with the train set) as he likes to play exclusively on his own. He does not voluntarily join in with messy activities … His concentration at story time is very short. He still finds it impossible to sit on the floor with other children for any length of time but will occasionally sit on the teacher's lap to listen for a short while.'

As happened so often throughout our work with Colin, casual observations like these provided guidelines for determining which behaviours to target. Professionals not trained in Behaviour Analysis recounted aspects of his behaviour as if 'that is just the way he is, and always will be' rather than viewing his behaviour as data upon which decisions could be based for designing appropriate interventions. In Colin's case this caused serious concern because these professionals would make far reaching decisions based upon their assessment (e.g., to place Colin in a Special Needs class). For us as therapists the race was on to ensure that Colin's behaviour developed in

1 2 3 4 5 6 7 8 9 10 11 12 13 14 15 16 17

the right direction so that future assessments by these professionals would show improvements that would lead to different decisions.

An important component of play behaviour is the ability to move from one toy to another as social interactions evolve across play time. Social interactions were difficult enough for Colin, but if he couldn't be flexible in his own play then how could he be flexible when other children made demands on him? Fixation on particular objects was therefore targeted for change. Laura had observed that Colin, once engaged in play with one particular toy, was unable to move from one play activity to another and back to the original activity. The intervention, therefore, was aimed at enabling Colin to become more flexible in play by being able to move between different toys upon request.

PROCEDURE

Colin and Laura were sitting on the kitchen floor. A range of toys were used, e.g., the doll's house, Lego®, toy box, or toy cars, etc. Different toys were used in each trial to ensure generalisation. One toy (Toy A) was given to Colin, another toy (Toy B) was placed on the other side of the room. Colin played with the first toy for approximately two minutes before Laura instructed him to go and play with the other toy. If Colin did not go to Toy B, Laura gave him

Receiving edible reinforcers

■ ■ ■ □ □ □ □ □ □ □ □ □ □ □ □ □ □

1 2 3 4 5 6 7 8 9 10 11 12 13 14 15 16 17

visual and physical cues, i.e., she showed Colin Toy B or took his hand and gently guided him to the new toy. Colin then played approximately for two minutes with this toy, before Laura instructed him to go back to Toy A. If Colin did not move, Laura gave him the same gentle prompts as before. Later, physical prompts were only used if it took more than 30 seconds for Colin to comply with verbal instructions.

Laura recorded three moves from Toy A to Toy B and three moves from Toy B back to Toy A as one session. For the behavioural measure Laura used the number (frequency) of instructions she gave to Colin before he complied.

During the second part of this intervention three sets of toys were used. Colin was seated on the kitchen floor, playing with one toy (Toy A). Another toy (Toy B) was placed in the adjacent living room and was out of Colin's sight and a third toy (Toy C) was placed on the other side of the kitchen. Colin played approximately two minutes with Toy A, Laura then gave him the instruction to move to Toy B which was placed in the living room. After Colin had played with Toy B for approximately two minutes, Laura instructed him to go and play with Toy C, which was placed in the kitchen. If Colin did not follow the instruction to move to the next toy, Laura went to the toy herself and instructed Colin to follow. The behavioural measure used was the latency (measured in seconds) with which Colin complied. Laura used edible and social reinforcers, such as Milkyway Stars®, hugs, and verbal praise.

RESULTS

Figures 4.7 and 4.8 show the results of this intervention. Figure 4.7 shows the number of times (frequency) Laura instructed Colin to move from playing with one toy to playing with another one before Colin complied.

Eight sessions were carried out. Each session averaged 19.6 minutes in duration. During the first four sessions the number of instructions for the move from Toy A to Toy B averaged 2.8 and the frequency of instruction to move from Toy B back to Toy A averaged 1. During the latter four sessions the number of instructions for the move from Toy A to Toy B averaged 1.5 and the frequency of instructions to move from Toy B back to Toy A averaged 1.7.

Figure 4.8 shows the latency with which Colin complied to the instruction to move from one toy to the next when tree toys were used.

Twelve trials were carried out. Each trial included three instructions; one for the move from Toy A to Toy B; one for the move from Toy B to Toy C; and

■ ■ ■ □ □ □ □ □ □ □ □ □ □ □ □ □ □
1 2 3 4 5 6 7 8 9 10 11 12 13 14 15 16 17

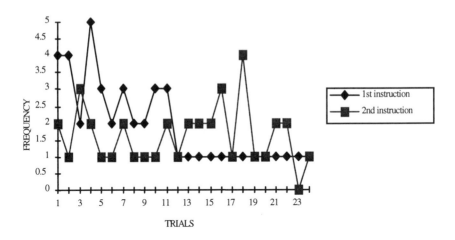

Figure 4.7 The frequency of instruction before Colin complied to verbal and visual cues when he was instructed to move from one activity to another (1st instruction) and back to the original activity (2nd instruction)

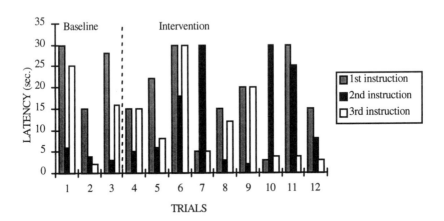

Figure 4.8 The latency with which Colin moved from Toy A to Toy B (1st instruction), from Toy B to Toy C (2nd instruction), and from Toy C to Toy A (3rd instruction)

one for the move from Toy C to Toy A. Overall, the latency with which Colin complied to the first instruction varied from under 5 seconds to 30 seconds and averaged 18 seconds. The latency for the second instruction varied from 2 seconds to 30 seconds and averaged 11 seconds. The latency for the third instruction varied from 2 to 30 seconds and averaged 12 seconds.

DISCUSSION

During this intervention Colin was instructed to move between toys. Initially two toys were used. The frequency of Laura's instruction before Colin complied was measured. It took an average of nearly three instructions before Colin moved between the toys, however, this soon reduced and Colin moved freely following verbal instructions. These trials were followed by trials involving three toys. Laura measured the latency with which Colin moved between these toys after being instructed to do so. Although the results of this intervention were varied, the overall latency with which Colin moved between the toys was relatively short.

During this intervention, data showed that Colin was doing a lot better than expected. He was, in fact, able to move between the toys quite freely. You may therefore wonder about the purpose of the intervention. There are a number of reasons why this was a useful exercise. First, although we did not assess his ability to move between three toys prior to the intervention we suspect that the training effect during the first part of this intervention (moving between two toys) probably enhanced his performance during the second part (moving between three toys). Second, this exercise showed Laura how to break down a task into small steps and it enabled her to see exactly what Colin could and could not do. This knowledge became extremely useful in later interventions. Third, it gave Colin the opportunity to practice behaviours that would help him integrate with his nursery school friends.

Laura noted an interesting point during this intervention: even after Colin had learned to move from one toy to the next, he often took an element of the first toy to the next toy, for example, he took a toy bear (Toy A) to the Lego® (Toy B), or if he had been pretending that the dolls in the Playmobile house (Toy A) were having breakfast, he continued to play 'having breakfast' with the puppets of TV characters Bert and Ernie (Toy B). In other words, while Colin complied with the request to move between the toys, he still engaged in aspects of the behaviour that Laura was trying to reduce, namely his fixation on particular objects. What should Laura have done? Should she have tried to

■ ■ ■ ☐ ☐ ☐ ☐ ☐ ☐ ☐ ☐ ☐ ☐ ☐ ☐ ☐ ☐

1   2   3   4   5   6   7   8   9   10 11 12 13 14 15 16 17

reduce the likelihood of this problem behaviour? In other words, should she have designed a procedure that would result in the behaviour being 'punished'.[2] An alternative to a punishment procedure would be to continue to ignore the problem behaviour and continue working on the original target behaviour (moving between toys). If attention had been the reinforcer the problem behaviour would be put on extinction while at the same time incompatible behaviours could be reinforced. Laura decided to opt for the latter. She continued to take a note of the incidence in which the problem behaviour occurred and continued to reinforce the behaviour of moving between toys. She found that the problem behaviour occurred less and less often until it eventually disappeared.

The term 'punishment' in this context needs further elaboration. Many people equate the term 'punishment' with aversive consequences, such as a smack, a fine, or imprisonment. In Applied Behaviour Analysis this term is defined very differently. The behaviour analytic definition of punishment is functional. A functional definition of punishment means that only consequences that *reduce* the likelihood of behaviour recurring are considered 'punishers'. As such a punisher could be anything: a hug is considered a punisher if it reduces crying, a reprimand is considered a punisher if it reduces sibling fighting.

The advantage of a properly conducted Behaviour Analysis is that parents are taught to rely on a functional analysis of the consequences that they arrange for their child's behaviour (see Chapter 3). They will, therefore, not use aversive consequences when non-aversive procedures are just as effective in reducing problem behaviours. The example of Laura's use of extinction combined with reinforcement of incompatible behaviours shows the positive results if an intervention is based on a functional analysis.

4. Target behaviour

Colin was now four years and one month old. The educational psychologist had carried out a language assessment on sub-tests of the British Ability Scales. He reported that expressive language was at circa three-year level (7th percentile) with receptive language less developed. Our next treatment

■ ■ ■ ■ □ □ □ □ □ □ □ □ □ □ □ □ □
1 2 3 4   6 7 8 9 10 11 12 13 14 15 16 17

---

2   In Applied Behaviour Analysis the term 'punishment' is a technical term that refers to consequences that reduce the likelihood of behaviour recurring (cf. Dillenburger and Keenan, 1995).

therefore focused on developing Colin's expressive and receptive language and expanding his sentences. A range of procedures were used during this stage of treatment. They will be introduced here in the sequence in which they took place.

FIRST PROCEDURE

Colin was seated at the table in the kitchen with a series of nine cards (from Masidlover and Knowles, 1979, Derbyshire Language Scheme: PERSON ACTION PLACE, depicting simple pen drawings, for example, a teddy bear sitting on a box) and was asked to give one of the cards to Laura. For example, Laura said 'Give me the teddy bear sitting on the box.' Colin had to hand the correct card to Laura and accompany his move by saying 'Here is the teddy bear sitting on the box'. He was then to ask for the next card himself, e.g., 'Give me the dolly sitting on the table'. Only complete sentences were reinforced using edible and social reinforcers such as Smarties® and praise. Edible reinforcers were faded as soon as possible and replaced with verbal praise.

RESULTS

Table 4.4 illustrates the results of the first procedure. Ticks indicate correct responding and crosses indicate incorrect responding. Colin answered 60% of Laura's requests correctly and phrased 100% of his requests to Laura correctly.

SECOND PROCEDURE

Colin and Laura (or one of Colin's sisters) were seated at the table in the kitchen. Derbyshire Language Cards and Tot's TV snap cards (pictures of children's television characters) were used. The cards were matched in pairs and placed face down on the table.

For Trials 1–9 two pairs (4 cards) were used, for Trials 10–12 five cards were used, and for Trials 13–27 three pairs (6 cards) were used. In turn Colin and Laura lifted one card and, without showing it to the other person, asked 'What have I got?' The other person had to say 'It's ...'. During Trials 1–10 correct 'guessing' was reinforced, during Trials 11–27 the use of full sentences was reinforced with edible and social reinforcers.

Two specific training sequences were included when Colin had problems with matching and naming the cards, e.g., when Laura said 'Are they [the two cards] the same?' and Colin responded by saying 'Are they the same?' The

■ ■ ■ ■ □ □ □ □ □ □ □ □ □ □ □ □ □

1 2 3 4 5 6 7 8 9 10 11 12 13 14 15 16 17

first training was aimed at modelling correct matching. This training was applied after the third trial. Four pairs of cards were placed face down on the table. Laura turned over one card asking Colin 'What's this card?' Colin had to reply 'That's the …' before the next card was turned around. When there were two cards lying face up Laura asked 'Are they the same?'. When he responded correctly it was Colin's turn to uncover the next two cards.

Table 4.4: Training expressive language		
Trial no.	Colin answers	Colin requests
1*	✗	✓
2*	✓	✓
3*	✗	✓
4*	✗	✓
5*	✗	✓
6*	✓	✓
7*	✗	✓
8**	✓	✓
9**	✓	✓
10**	✓	✓
11**	✓	✓
12**	✓	✓
13**	✓	✓
14**	✓	✓
15**	✓	✓
16**	✓	✓

*   First session
**   Second session

The second training sequence was introduced after Trial 22 in order to teach Colin to distinguish between one person asking a question and another answering. The family game of 'Snap' was introduced. For this game each

1 2 3 4 5 6 7 8 9 10 11 12 13 14 15 16 17

player received the same number of cards and, in turn, put one card openly in the middle of the table. If the card matched the card that was put in the middle of the table by the previous player, all players were to shout 'Snap'. The player who shouted first got all the cards that were in the middle of the table. This sequence was repeated until one player had all the cards. During the training sequence Colin, Laura, and other members of the family played 'Snap' and each player named the card they were playing (e.g., saying 'This is a teddy') and all players confirmed with 'Yes it is' or 'No it isn't.' Laura sometimes deliberately named the cards wrongly and Colin had to say 'No it isn't' or 'Yes it is.'

Matching cards

RESULTS

Table 4.5 shows the results of the second procedure. Ticks indicate correct responding and crosses indicate incorrect responding. Colin responded correctly in 89% of trials in which he had to answer Laura's question 'What have I got?' He responded 93% correct in trials in which he had to ask/request.

■ ■ ■ ■ □ □ □ □ □ □ □ □ □ □ □ □ □

1 2 3 4 5 6 7 8 9 10 11 12 13 14 15 16 17

Table 4.5: Guessing and matching cards			
Trial no.	No. of cards	Colin answers	Colin requests
1*	4	✓	✓
2*	4	✓	✓
3*	4	✓	✓
4*	4	✓	✓
5*	4	✗	✗
6*	4	✓	✗
7*	4	✓	✓
8*	4	✗	✓
9*	4	✓	✓
10**	5	✓	✓
11**	5	✓	✓
12**	5	✓	✓
13**	6	✓	✓
14**	6	✓	✓
15**	6	✓	✓
16**	6	✓	✓
17**	6	✓	✓
18**	6	✓	✓
19**	6	✓	✓
20**	6	✓	✓
21**	6	✓	✓
22**	6	✓	✓
23**	6	✓	✓
24**	6	✓	✓
25**	6	✓	✓
26**	6	✓	✓
27**	6	✓	✓

*   correct 'guessing' was reinforced
**   correct sentences were reinforced

1   2   3   4   5   6   7   8   9   10 11 12 13 14 15 16 17

DISCUSSION

Two procedures were devised to improve Colin's expressive language. During the first procedure results show that Colin responded correctly in the majority of tasks requiring him to use increasingly complex sentences. During the second procedure a number of problems were noted. Two additional training procedures were included: the matching game and the naming game.

The introduction of additional training games was very important in this intervention. When Colin was unable to complete a task correctly, Laura did not simply resign herself to the fact that 'he just cannot do it' but developed interesting and fun ways to deal with the problem. Colin enjoyed these additional training sequences and given that the whole family took part, he probably learned much more than just the matching or naming of cards. Laura had shown that she was beginning to design interventions by herself. She was no longer completely dependent on the behaviour analysts to design the intervention. She had used her own initiative and creativity to help her child. This was very encouraging. It showed that Laura had made good use of the behaviour analytic parent training over the past three or four months. It also showed that in order to help Colin she did not need elaborate materials. All she needed was her newly acquired knowledge and understanding and the motivation and encouragement to apply this to her work with Colin.

Improvements were also reflected in the speech and language therapist's report:

> '*Attention/Listening skills:* There have been significant improvements in this area over the past 4 months. Previously [Colin] found it difficult to attend to adult directed table-top activities for more than a few minutes. However, he will now concentrate for periods of 20–25 minutes in a one-to-one situation with little prompting.'

5. Target behaviour

The educational psychologist reported that Colin still engaged in '…a good deal of echolalia and repetitive expression'. Colin's echolalia took the following form. When, for example, Laura showed him a toy train and gave him the instruction 'say train', Colin responded by saying 'say train', rather than by saying 'train'. The target behaviour was for Colin to repeat the name of an object only, thus omitting the instruction 'say'. The dependant measure during this treatment was the frequency of Colin's correct responses.

■ ■ ■ ■ ■ □ □ □ □ □ □ □ □ □ □ □ □
1 2 3 4 5 6 7 8 9 10 11 12 13 14 15 16 17

PROCEDURE

Colin was seated at a table opposite Laura. Laura said 'say apple', 'say biscuit', etc. using twelve different words (see Table 4.6). When Colin responded correctly (one word phrase) Laura gave verbal reinforcers ('Well done', 'That's right', 'Good'). This procedure was repeated on the same day with Colin and three other children. Three days later the procedure was repeated again.

The procedure was adjusted after these three trials because the results were discouraging. Ten words were used. Laura or one of Colin's older sisters said 'ball' and Colin had to repeat 'ball'. She then said 'say ball' and the correct response was 'ball'. This procedure was carried out with Colin alone and, three days later, with Colin and one other child. Verbal reinforcers were given for correct responses.

Table 4.6: Assessing verbal repetition of instruction			
	Trial 1	**Trial 2**	**Trial 3**
Instruction	Colin alone	Colin + three others	Colin + three others
say train	✗	✗	✗
say man	✓	✗	✗
say go	✓	✓	✗
say sock	✗	✗	✗
say ball	✓	✗	✗
say train set	✓	✗	✗
say nose	✓	✗	✗
say slipper	✓	✓	✗
say scarf	✓	✓	✓
say cup	✗	✗	✓
say tractor	✓	✓	✗
say car	✓	✓	✗

RESULTS

Tables 4.6 and 4.7 show the results of this procedure. Table 4.6 shows the rates of correct responding during the first condition. Ticks indicate correct

1 2 3 4 5 6 7 8 9 10 11 12 13 14 15 16 17

responding while crosses indicate times when Colin included the instruction 'say' in his response. Colin responded correctly to 75% of the instructions during the first trial; however, his performance deteriorated during Trial 2 and 3 to 41% and 9% respectively.

Table 4.7 shows the results of the adjusted procedure. During the two trials that were carried out Colin responded correctly 90% and 88.8% of the time.

Table 4.7: Training correct verbal repetition of instruction			
First day		Three days later	
Instruction	Colin alone	Instruction	Colin + one other
ball	✓	ball	✓
grass	✓	hat	✓
rabbit	✓	stop	✓
daddy	✓	say stop	✓
Mummy	✓	elephant	✓
fire engine	✓	say elephant	✓
penguin	✓	fish	✓
say penguin	✓	say fish	✗
dog	✓	dog	✓
say dog	✗	say dog	✓
giraffe	✓	daddy	✓
say giraffe	✓	say daddy	✓
elephant	✓	boat	✓
say elephant	✓	say boat	✓
lion	✓	seaside	✓
say lion	✓	say seaside	✗
panda	✓	lorry	✓
say panda	✓	say lorry	✓
tiger	✓		
say tiger	✗		

■ ■ ■ ■ ■ □ □ □ □ □ □ □ □ □ □ □ □
1 2 3 4 5 6 7 8 9 10 11 12 13 14 15 16 17

DISCUSSION

A procedure was developed to deal with Colin's echolalia and repetitive expression. Colin was given the instruction to say a single word. Initially Colin repeated the instruction 'say' together with the single word. A procedure was developed in which Laura, or one of Colin's older sisters, said the single word initially on its own and then paired it with the instruction 'say'. This procedure resulted in Colin responding correctly in the majority of cases.

This procedure offers a good example for data-based decision making. Laura had taken data on Colin's responding throughout the early trials and found that the number of correct responses did not increase. In fact they seemed to decrease. Instead of continuing an intervention that was obviously not working she weighed up the following alternatives: (1) she could change the words she was using; (2) she could ask the other children to deliberately respond wrongly; or (3) she could break the task down into smaller steps. The third option seemed the most appropriate and the procedure was adjusted accordingly. The results of the adjusted procedure showed the effectiveness of this adjustment.

6. Target behaviour

The speech and language therapist reported that '...[Colin's] eye contact has improved'. However, she observed that 'Occasionally he will avoid eye contact, primarily if he is finding an activity or task difficult'. Although eye contact had been targeted during earlier interventions the latency with which Colin made eye contact had increased and it was important to focus on Colin's eye contact again. Measurements were taken on latency and on generalisation of eye contact.

PROCEDURE

Colin was in the kitchen playing with three girls, his sister and her two friends. The girls called Colin's name in turn and used verbal praise when Colin made eye contact with them. The latency with which Colin made eye contact with each of the girls was measured during this procedure.

RESULTS

Figure 4.9 shows the latency with which Colin made eye contact with the girls during six trials.

1   2   3   4   5   6   7   8   9   10 11 12 13 14 15 16 17

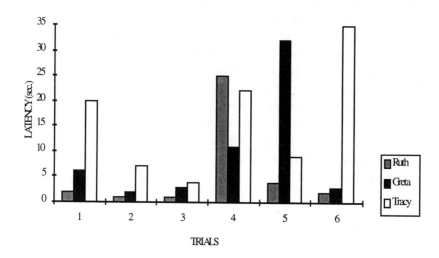

Figure 4.9 The latency with which Colin made eye contact with three different girls following the prompt 'Colin'

All the trials took place during the same session. The latency for Colin's sister Ruth averaged 5.8 seconds, while the latency for her friend Greta averaged 9.5 seconds. The average latency for Tracy was 16.2 seconds.

DISCUSSION

This intervention was designed to decrease the latency with which Colin made eye contact after being called by his name and to ensure that this behaviour generalised to other people.

Although social isolation and social distancing are frequent features of autism the results of this intervention indicate that Colin clearly differentiated in the way he related to each of the girls. Laura commented that the results reflect Colin's general affection for each of the girls; Ruth is Colin's sister and they have a very good relationship; Greta had always been close to Colin, carrying him when he was a baby, feeding him, and helping to change him; Colin's relationship with Tracy is good but she is 'bossier' than he likes.

7. Target behaviour

This intervention took place when Colin was four years and two months old. Colin's speech had first been addressed in Interventions 4 and 5. While these interventions resulted in some very basic improvements, the Speech and Language therapist still reported that '[Colin] presents with severely disordered communication development. His attention to communication directed at him is variable. Echolalia is also present ... Sometimes after repetition he will then provide an appropriate answer.' Clearly, more work was necessary. The dependent measure during this treatment, therefore, was 'fluency' of Colin's speech (see Appendix 1 and 2). Fluency was measured as a percentage of trial duration during which Colin told a story without verbal prompts to continue.

PROCEDURE

This training procedure took place in a variety of places, including the kitchen and the car. Colin was asked to tell familiar children's stories ('Three Billy Goats Gruff', 'The Three Little Pigs', or 'Goldilocks'). Colin was prompted to continue the story when the flow of his story telling faltered. The duration of trials, the frequency of verbal prompts, and the duration of interruptions were measured.

Story telling

■ ■ ■ ■ ■ ■ ■ □ □ □ □ □ □ □ □ □ □
1   2   3   4   5   6   7   8   9   10 11 12 13 14 15 16 17

RESULTS

Table 4.8 illustrates the results obtained during nine trials. Each trial lasted for an average of 5 minutes and an average of 14 verbal prompts were give per trial. This meant that each trial was interrupted for an average of 47 seconds. Overall the fluency of story telling averaged 85.3 % of trial duration.

Table 4.8: Training fluency of speech during story telling				
Number of trial and Name of story	Duration of trial (minutes)	Verbal prompts (frequency)	Duration of interruption (seconds)	Fluent story telling (% of trial duration)
1. Three Billy Goats Gruff	5 m	14	35 s	88.4%
2. Three Billy Goats Gruff	4 m 35 s	16	no data	no data
3. Three Little Pigs	4 m	20	no data	no data
4. Three Billy Goats Gruff	3 m 30 s	11	33 s	84.3%
5. Three Little Pigs	5 m 25 s	21	64 s	80.0%
6. Three Little Pigs	6 m 35 s	13	50 s	87.2%
7. Three Little Pigs	6 m 30 s	9	29 s	92.6%
8. Goldilocks	5 m 30 s	12	81 s	76.2%
9. Goldilocks	5 m 40 s	10	38 s	88.9%

DISCUSSION

This treatment concentrated on fluency of Colin's speech. Colin was asked to tell familiar children's stories to Laura. Laura offered verbal prompts to encourage continued story telling whenever Colin hesitated or faltered. During the final trials most of the interruptions were prompts at the beginning of the story. Once Colin was in the flow of talking he required fewer prompts. Repeated story telling of familiar children's stories led to improved fluency of speech without the use of extra reinforcers.

The aim of extending the fluency of Colin's language was achieved by encouraging him to participate increasingly in telling his favourite stories. Although the stories were familiar Colin had different experiences with each

1 2 3 4 5 6 7 8 9 10 11 12 13 14 15 16 17

of them. For example, the first story ('The Billy Goats Gruff') had been used in another procedure when the duration of eye contact was targeted and Laura had been the main story teller, Colin had only occasionally contributed. The story of 'The Three Little Pigs', for example, had only recently been re-discovered in a story book. The version used during this intervention was not an interpretation with which Colin was familiar. The story of 'Goldilocks' was a story Colin had listened to in the past but he had never actively participated in telling it before.

There was a clear increase in fluency of story telling for 'The Three Little Pigs'; the percentage of trial duration during which Colin fluently told the story increased between Trials 5, 6, and 7 from 80% to 92.6%. There was also an increase in fluency for the story of 'Goldilocks' during Trials 8 and 9 where the duration of fluent story telling increased from 76.2% to 88.9% of trial duration. It can therefore be said that with practice Colin's fluency of story telling increased. In this procedure no extrinsic reinforcers were used. The 'fun of telling a story' functioned effectively as an intrinsic reinforcer for fluency of speech. It was encouraging to observe that four months into treatment Colin was beginning to respond to 'intrinsic' reinforcement.

8. Target behaviour

This intervention targeted a complex behaviour often referred to as object permanence. Developmental psychologists have observed that before the age of eight to nine months a baby's gaze does not follow a toy that falls from their high chair or that is deliberately hidden from their view. After that age babies usually follow the toy with their gaze and try to retrieve the toy. Colin did not do this. Once a toy was removed he did not follow it either with his gaze nor did he try to retrieve it. A procedure was therefore devised that would teach Colin to engage in these behaviours.

PROCEDURE

Colin was seated at the table in the utility room. A total of six toys (a toy purse, a toy car, a jigsaw puzzle of the toy character 'Noddy', a small book set, a toy telephone, and an alphabet jigsaw puzzle) were used for this intervention. Each toy was used for a total of five trials. During each trial the toy was first given to Colin and then removed. Each time a toy was removed Laura took a note of Colin's response. She noted whether or not Colin

followed the toy with his gaze (look) or whether he reached out for the toy (touch).

Trials 1–3 were used as 'baseline'. Laura did nothing to encourage Colin's pursuit of the toys. Laura then showed Colin how to play with each of the toys (modelling), i.e., she showed Colin what was in the purse or how Noddy's car door opened. She let Colin play with the toy for a brief moment. The toy was then removed for two further trials and Laura noted Colin's response.

RESULTS

Figure 4.10 shows results achieved during this intervention with six different toys. There was a marked increase in Colin's ability to follow each of the six toys with his gaze after Laura modelled functional play. Colin looked at all the toys after this and touched all of them apart from the toy telephone.

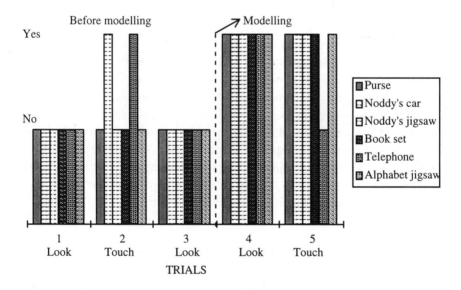

Figure 4.10 The incidence with which Colin looked at or touched a range of toys after they had been removed for brief periods, before and after his mother modelled functional play with each toy

DISCUSSION

A procedure was devised that successfully taught Colin to show continued interest in toys once they were removed from him. The baseline indicated a very low level of object permanence; however, after the intervention (modelling), Colin's object permanence increased and he pursued all the toys by looking and touching, with the exception of the toy telephone, which he did not touch. Following this intervention Laura reported that Colin got very interested in the book set and called 'Hi, books' if someone took them. Laura commented that in the days following this intervention Colin continued to play with all the toys that had been used during this intervention.

This procedure is of particular interest to developmental psychologists, because in the past object permanence was considered a concept that develops more or less as part of maturation and is generally considered to be genetically controlled. The fact that modelling can be used to teach these behaviours indicates that learning plays a major part in the development of object permanence (see Dillenburger and Keenan, 1997).

9. Target behaviour

The focus of this treatment was once again on Colin's echolalia. Colin still frequently repeated what was said to him. Sometimes the correct response followed the repetition, at other times he just repeated the whole question without an appropriate response. Earlier interventions (Interventions 4, 5 and 7) had focused on basic language skills, but more work was needed. Laura discussed the details of Colin's language development with his Speech and Language therapist who was very supportive (see Appendix 3). The aim of this procedure was to facilitate Colin's discrimination of appropriate and inappropriate responses to questions. We knew that there were occasions when he could use appropriate answers, but he did not do this consistently.

PROCEDURE

Colin was seated at a table. Speech therapy tasks were used for this intervention. Following the completion of the speech therapy task, Colin was asked a range of questions related to the completed task. The questions were asked either in the presence of a green or a red card. Our intention was to use these cards to facilitate his discrimination of appropriate responding. However, the cards by themselves would not do this. There needed to be consequences for appropriate and inappropriate responding. When Laura

1 2 3 4 5 6 7 8 9 10 11 12 13 14 15 16 17

showed the green card Colin was reinforced for echolalic responding, i.e., repeating the question. When Laura showed the red card he was reinforced for correct responding, i.e., answering the question.

Initially trials incorporated approximately 7–10 questions. This was slowly increased to 60 questions during the final trials. During Trial 1 red and green cards were presented randomly. During Trials 2–16 red and green cards were presented alternatively (50% of trials each). During Trials 17–21 green cards were faded, i.e., used much less frequently (25% of trials). Generalisation trials were carried out by Colin's father.

It would not be socially acceptable, or practical, for Laura to carry around a set of green and red cards to help Colin converse appropriately. We needed to find a way to replace the cards with other socially acceptable cues. During Trials 29–34 the prefix 'well' was used with the questions in the presence of the red card and the prefix 'so' was used in the presence of the green card. For example, instead of asking 'What did Teddy do?' the question was 'Well, what did teddy do?', or 'So, what did teddy do?'. Echolalic responding was reinforced when the prefix 'so' was used. When the prefix 'well' was used correct responding was reinforced, i.e., answering the question. After Trial 34 the cards were no longer used. The prefixes were then gradually withdrawn.

Tokens (i.e., toy coins) were used as reinforcers. In order to establish a 'token economy',[3] Colin initially received tokens for accomplishing his speech therapy exercises. Later, during the intervention Colin earned tokens for appropriate responses. After this, earning tokens became progressively more difficult. At the end of each session Colin exchanged the tokens for something from a 'shop' that Laura had set up as part of the token economy. In the event he usually chose chocolates, either M'n'M's® or Milkyway Stars®.

1 2 3 4 5 6 7 8 9 10 11 12 13 14 15 16 17

3   A token economy is simply a system whereby tokens are given as consequences for appropriate behaviour. Tokens can be exchanged later for either a privilege (e.g., watching T.V.) or in Colin's case, sweets. With this system you can deliver tokens immediately without interrupting a session to wait for consumption of an edible reinforcer. You also can require an increase in behaviour before a token is given. Additionally, you can raise the 'price' of an item to be 'purchased' with tokens thereby requiring more behaviour per reinforcer.

RESULTS

Figure 4.11 shows the results of 53 trials. The baseline showed that Colin did not respond consistently in the presence of either the red or the green card. During the initial training phase his appropriate responding to the red card (answering the question) was reinforced and increased to near 100%. He was also reinforced for responding appropriately to the green card (echolalic responses) and correct responding increased to about 50% of the time. During the fading phase, when green cards were used less frequently, Colin maintained the high rate of correct responding to red cards. During the generalisation phase in which Colin's father worked with Colin, the rate of correct responding to both red and green cards decreased slightly, however, correct responding increased again when Laura paired the cards with prefixes. Finally when the prefixes were faded and withdrawn echolalic responding disappeared.

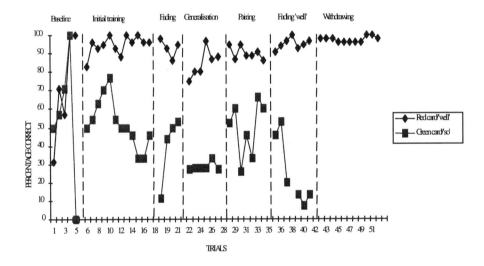

Figure 4.11 The percentage of correct responses to questions asked in the presence of the RED card and (non-echolalic responses reinforced) and in the presence of the GREEN card (echolalic responses reinforced)

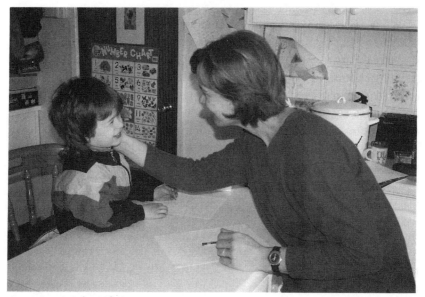

Receiving social reinforcers

DISCUSSION

A procedure was devised to eliminate echolalic responding to questions. In the presence of a green card echolalic responding was reinforced while in the presence of a red card correct responding was reinforced. The cards were then replaced by verbal prefixes to the questions, which were gradually faded until Colin answered all questions correctly. Data show the elimination of echolalia over 53 trials.

Earlier we discussed the importance of an A–B–C analysis in designing a treatment procedure (Chapters 1 and 3). Up to now we have mainly concentrated on the effects of consequences (reinforcers) on behaviour. In this intervention we had a good example of how antecedents can effectively be used to change behaviour. First we trained a certain (undesired) behaviour in the presence of a certain stimulus (echolalic responding in the presence of the green card/prefix 'so') and another (desired) behaviour in the presence of another stimulus (non-echolalic responding in the presence of a red card/ prefix 'well'). We then faded the stimulus to which the undesired behaviour was trained and found that Colin engaged in the undesired behaviour less often.

■ ■ ■ ■ ■ ■ ■ ■ ■ □ □ □ □ □ □ □ □

1 2 3 4 5 6 7 8 9 10 11 12 13 14 15 16 17

While this procedure sounds straightforward the intervention reported here shows that it is not as simple as it first appears. For example, the training should be carried out until the undesirable behaviour is reliably under stimulus control; in our case that would have meant until Colin reliably engaged in echolalic responding in the presence of the green card/prefix 'so'. A problem arose when early in the procedure Colin responded to the green card questions with correct answers rather than echolalic responses. Laura was faced with a dilemma. According to the procedure she should not have reinforced this behaviour, however, since this was our final target behaviour it was difficult for her to ignore it and she did reinforce it. This meant that discriminative control by the green card was never at 100%. She therefore decided quite early on (after only 12 trials) to use the green card less often than originally planned (25% of the time rather than 50% of the time).

This procedure was one of the most work intensive interventions during the first year of Applied Behaviour Analysis with Colin. There were many occasions when Laura was tired and nearly gave up the intervention. Laura's perseverance with the work was eventually rewarded by success. However, it showed that although some of the earlier procedures seemed to be effective very quickly some behavioural excesses or deficits are much more difficult to deal with.

10. Target behaviour

Colin was four years two months old when this intervention took place. We were now four months into treatment. The educational psychologist had administered the Merrill-Palmer Test and reported:

> [Colin] was successful on 75% of tests within the 30–35 months range and 66% of tests within the 36–41 months range. He failed on all verbal tests with the exception of 'Repetition of Words' within the 18–24 months range. His overall performance placed him at 10th percentile level, bordering below and low average. It should be noted that the Merrill-Palmer Test tends to inflate ability when related to tests used at a later age.

There are two ways to handle this information. One way, the one that is traditionally taught, is to accept the outcome as a fait accompli. That is to say, this is all that Colin can do, God love him! The other way, the behavioural way, is to treat these findings as a baseline measure and see how much can be

■ ■ ■ ■ ■ ■ ■ ■ ■ □ □ □ □ □ □ □ □
1 2 3 4 5 6 7 8 9 10 11 12 13 14 15 16 17

changed. This next intervention was designed in order to establish two-way verbal communication.

PROCEDURE

Colin was seated on the floor in the sitting room or in the kitchen. Laura placed a 24–piece floor jigsaw puzzle in front of him. He was given the verbal instruction to complete the jigsaw puzzle as fast as possible. A stopwatch was placed within his sight. Colin then had to ask for pieces of the puzzle by verbally describing them, e.g., 'The piece with Sooty's ear', 'The piece of crab in the bucket', 'The piece of Sooty's foot' etc. Initially Laura described the details of the piece he needed, later he had to ask for and then describe the piece she was holding. Before each piece was handed to Colin he had to establish eye contact. Laura, Geoffrey, and Colin's friends carried out this procedure with him.

In a similar procedure that was carried out around the same time Colin was seated at a table and asked to complete 6– and 7–piece jigsaw puzzles. This time Laura hid the jigsaw puzzle pieces behind her back or in her hand. Colin had to ask for each of the pieces before he got it. Verbal praise was used as the reinforcer. Eye contact was required. Initially Colin's sister modelled the procedure. Again Colin was told to work as fast as possible and a stopwatch was placed within his sight.

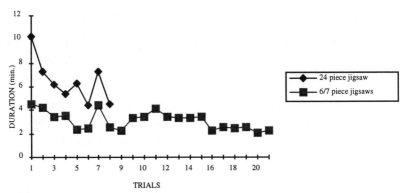

Figure 4.12 Time taken to complete jigsaw puzzles when Colin had to ask for and describe each piece before placing it into the puzzle

RESULTS

Figure 4.12 illustrates the results of both procedures. Eight trials were carried out using the first procedure with the 24–piece floor jigsaw puzzle. While

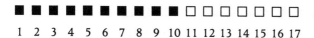

Colin needed over ten minutes during the first trial to complete the puzzle this reduced to just under five minutes in the last trial. During Trial 5 the downward trend in the data was interrupted, Colin was very distractable on this day. Again the downward trend in the data was interrupted on Trial 7 when Colin had a cold and took a lot longer than usual to slot the jigsaw pieces together.

DISCUSSION

Two procedures were devised to increase verbal two-way communication with Colin. He was to complete a range of jigsaw puzzles by asking Laura, Geoffrey, or a friend for each piece, i.e., describing each piece, before slotting it into its place. Results indicate that Colin was able to complete the task with increasing speed, showing that his verbal communication skills became increasingly effective. In other words, he was learning to make language a useful tool.

11. Target behaviour

This intervention focused again on Colin's eye contact. Since the initial training of eye contact this behaviour had become a part requirement of almost all the other procedures. However, at the time of this intervention, Colin needed a number of prompts before making eye contact. The educational psychologist reported that during testing Colin

> '...required frequent prompting to attend. When the activity was not novel one could fleetingly gain eye contact, but if [Colin] was not instructed to 'look at my eyes' and reinforced, eye contact was lost.'

This intervention was therefore designed to elicit eye contact after one prompt only. Furthermore, Colin had to make eye contact when many distractions, such as intense play with siblings, were present.

PROCEDURE

Colin was seated at a table and engaged in a variety of activities, such as playing with Lego® with his sister, completing jigsaw puzzles, or playing with other toys. Laura or Geoffrey, called Colin's name once, and when Colin made eye contact he received edible reinforcers, such as sweets, and verbal reinforcers, such as his parent saying 'good boy'. The procedure was conducted initially in four sessions (10 to 15 trials each) and five months later

1 2 3 4 5 6 7 8 9 10 11 12 13 14 15 16 17

this was followed up with three sessions (10 trials each). The latency with which Colin made eye contact was used to measure the effectiveness of this intervention.

RESULTS

Figure 4.13 shows the results of this intervention. The latency with which Colin made eye contact initially increased from an average of 7.8 seconds (during the first session) to 13.7 seconds and 23.4 seconds (during Sessions 2 and 3 respectively). During Session 4 the latency decreased to an average of 3.5 seconds. At follow-up this low latency was maintained during three sessions (average latency 4.7 seconds, 1.4 seconds, and 3.1 seconds).

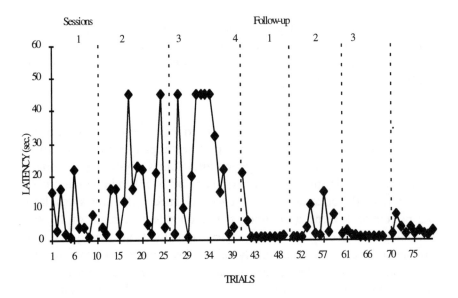

Figure 4.13 The latency with which Colin made eye contact when his father or mother called his name once only while he was playing intensely (initial training and five months follow-up training)

■ ■ ■ ■ ■ ■ ■ ■ ■ ■ □ □ □ □ □ □ □

1 2 3 4 5 6 7 8 9 10 11 12 13 14 15 16 17

DISCUSSION

A procedure was implemented that focused on decreasing the latency with which Colin made eye contact when his name was called once, while he was busy playing. Data show that a reduction of the latency was achieved during the initial four training sessions. This reduction was maintained at five months follow-up.

Once a behaviour is trained successfully it can revert back to its original level if maintenance contingencies are not arranged carefully. In Colin's case we saw how despite the large amount of work being carried out during the initial interventions (Interventions 1 and 6) his ability to make and maintain eye contact had deteriorated. The importance of continual checks to ensure that the behaviour that was once trained is in fact still reliably performed under the appropriate circumstances can not be understated.

12. Target behaviour

Although Colin was making eye contact after one verbal prompt only, this contact was at times fleeting and short-lived. This intervention, known as 'the looking game', therefore focused on extending the duration of eye contact.

PROCEDURE

This procedure was carried out in various locations inside and outside Colin's home. All members of the family took part (see Appendix 4 for a record of how the 'looking game' was integrated into Colin's day-to-day activities). Colin was seated facing the other person and both looked into each other's eyes. Initially the duration of eye contact was timed with a stopwatch, later the players took turns at counting the seconds (e.g., a count of 10 was considered 10 seconds of eye contact). Initially Colin was physically prompted, for example, Laura gently held his head or shoulders to ensure he was looking at her. When Colin was able to maintain eye contact for the specified time, the duration for which Colin was to hold eye contact (the 'criterion') was slowly increased (in increments of 5 or 10 seconds). Social and verbal reinforcers were used, such as hugs and smiles, and 'Good', or 'Well done'. Activity reinforcers were also used: Colin was allowed to play with favoured toys (e.g., the computer) or engage in favourite activities (e.g., going outside to play) after doing looking exercises. These reinforcers were delivered only when he had reached the specific criterion on each occasion.

1   2   3   4   5   6   7   8   9   10 11 12 13 14 15 16 17

RESULTS

Figure 4.14 shows the results achieved during the 'looking game'. Following the baseline, the aim (criterion) was that Colin would hold eye contact for 10 seconds. This was achieved quickly. The criterion was therefore increased to 15 seconds but had to be reduced again to 10 seconds after a few trials when the data showed that Colin was unable to hold eye contact for as long as 15 seconds. After Trial 65 the criterion was raised again and this time Colin was able to hold eye contact for 15 seconds consistently. After Trial 85 the criterion was therefore increased to 20 seconds and after a few trials it was raised to 30 seconds. By Trial 95 the criterion was raised to 50 seconds. This meant that only eye contact that lasted 50 seconds was reinforced. As can be seen in Figure 4.14 data showed that Colin was not able to hold eye contact for 50 seconds consistently. Laura therefore reduced the criterion to 30 seconds before she raised it to 40 seconds for the remainder of the intervention.

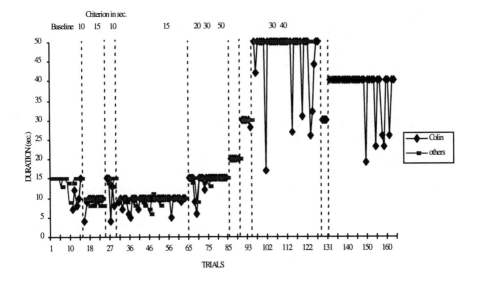

Figure 4.14 The duration with which Colin played the 'Looking game' with others while the criterion was adjusted depending on his performance

■ ■ ■ ■ ■ ■ ■ ■ ■ ■ ■ □ □ □ □ □ □

1 2 3 4 5 6 7 8 9 10 11 12 13 14 15 16 17

DISCUSSION

A procedure was devised to increase the duration of Colin's eye contact. By increasing the criterion gradually the duration of eye contact was increased from 10 seconds to 40 seconds.

A number of important points became apparent during this intervention. Much of Colin's training had been carried out in situations that were deliberately held quiet and without interruption. This was important especially during the early trials in order to establish the training routine. Some behaviours must be trained first before they can be transferred into everyday activities. The 'looking game', once established, was played in much more natural settings. School holidays had begun at Trial 107. This meant that trials could not be held in quiet circumstances anymore, as other children came in or walked through the treatment room. Data show that the criterion was not consistently reached under these circumstances. There were some other problems, for example, it was difficult to record data under these circumstances and consequently data were not always recorded. The problem with not recording data is that there is no early detection of an intervention that is not effective.

Another big problem was the timing of the game with the stopwatch. Colin found this very distracting. It was therefore decided to use counting and a count of 10 was recorded as 10 seconds duration. This was much easier and had the advantage that Colin could count himself and thus take control of the game.

During the looking game it became apparent that Colin frequently avoided the task. For example, he initially counted very loudly (without eye contact) and fidgeted, thereby avoiding lengthy eye contact. Consequently Laura ignored him (i.e., she put task avoidance behaviours on extinction) until he made eye contact. She then immediately began to count and Colin joined in.

In the early stages of the looking game, when Colin did not make eye contact, Laura used physical prompting. She put her hands gently over Colin's eyes and slowly moved her hand down to direct his attention. Colin usually made eye contact after this kind of physical prompt. Physical prompts can often be useful tools especially during the early part of the intervention. Laura also used them in order to reduce verbal instructions to a minimum. It is however, important to remember to phase physical prompts out as soon as

■ ■ ■ ■ ■ ■ ■ ■ ■ ■ ■ ■ □ □ □ □ □
1 2 3 4 5 6 7 8 9 10 11 12 13 14 15 16 17

possible, and to ensure that the target behaviour is reached without physical prompts.

During this intervention Laura used activity reinforcers. Laura had established earlier that Colin responded to activity reinforcers particularly well. She purchased a small toy truck. This toy was not made available to Colin during the day; however, he could earn playtime with this new toy by achieving criterion in the looking game. This worked so well that Colin initiated the looking game simply by getting the folder in which Laura recorded the results and placing it on the table.

The looking game was another good example of data-based decision making. Laura recorded the duration for which Colin made eye contact and used this information to decide when to raise the criterion. If she found that Colin did not meet the criterion she reduced it until the data showed that Colin was making eye contact consistently; only then was the criterion raised again.

13. Target behaviour

There had been definite improvements in the duration with which Colin made eye contact. However, the looking game was a rather arbitrary way of achieving lengthy duration of eye contact. The next intervention was therefore designed to increase duration of eye contact during story telling, an activity that parents and teachers do frequently with children and during which children are expected to look at the parent or teacher who is telling the story. This intervention was aimed at 'normalising' Colin's behaviour in this respect.

PROCEDURES

Colin was seated at a table facing Laura. He was instructed to look at Laura while she was telling him a children's story. Whenever Colin looked away, i.e., when eye contact ceased, Laura stopped telling the story. When Colin re-established eye contact she continued telling the story. Most of the stories were familiar to Colin ('Goldilocks and the Three Bears', 'The Three Little Pigs', 'The Three Billy Goats Gruff'). However, a new story ('Little Red Riding Hood') was also used.

Maintenance training was carried out in daily living situations using naturally occurring reinforcement opportunities. This meant that after the training any of Colin's requests had to be accompanied with eye contact

before he got what he had requested. For example, when Colin asked for a drink or snack, or to be allowed to go out or play, he had to make eye contact before he was given permission.

Table 4.9: Training eye contact during story telling				
Number of trial and name of story	Duration of trial (minutes)	Loss of eye contact (frequency)	Loss of eye contact (seconds)	Eye contact (% of trial duration)
1. Goldilocks	11 m	6	32 s	95.5 %
2. Three Little Pigs	8 m	15	52 s	83.8%
3. Three Billy Goats Gruff	4 m 20 s	7	18 s	93.1%
4. Goldilocks	8 m	2	18 s	96.3%
5. Three Billy Goats Gruff	4 m	7	24 s	90.0%
6. Little Red Riding Hood	4 m	6	34 s	84.5%
7. Three Billy Goats Gruff	4 m 30 s	1	7 s	97.0%
8. Goldilocks	3 m 20 s	6	33 s	84%
9. Little Red Riding Hood	4 m	5	11 s	95.4%
10. Little Red Riding Hood	4 m 20 s	0	0	100%
11. Little Red Riding Hood	4 m 25 s	4	9 s	96.6%
12. Little Red Riding Hood	4 m 12 s	0	0	100%

RESULTS

Table 4.9 shows the results achieved with the story telling game. In all, twelve trials were completed. Four different stories were used. Trial duration averaged 5.2 minutes and an average of 4.9 interruptions were made in each trial due to loss of eye contact. Consequently, an average of 19.8 seconds were lost in each trial. It is interesting to note that there was a clear difference in the duration of eye contact between the most favourite story ('Goldilocks') and a much less liked story ('Three Little Pigs') (95.5% vs. 83.8%). These stories were used in Trials 1 and 2. In Trial 4 there was a return to 'Goldilocks' which resulted in slightly improved performance (95.5% vs. 96.3%). However, this improvement was not maintained in Trial 8 when Goldilocks

was used again (84%). The new story ('Little Red Riding Hood') was used five times (Trials 6, 9, 10, 11, 12). A steady improvement in Colin's performance was recorded in relation to this story (84.5%, 95.4%, 100%, 96.6%, and 100%).

DISCUSSION

During 12 trials of story telling eye contact was measured in terms of frequency of loss of eye contact as well as duration of time spent engaged in eye contact. By and large the duration for which Colin held eye contact during story telling was relatively high. The only exception was during a story that was considered unpopular from the outset ('The Three Little Pigs'). It was interesting to note that this lack of popularity was actually reflected in lack of eye contact. Although in general eye contact was maintained for over 80% of story telling time, there was an indication that with repetition of the same story this could be improved.

Laura reported that a major problem was to note the measurement while at the same time attempting to tell the story and maintaining eye contact. This problem was remedied after the first trial by getting Geoffrey to record. During some of the trials when the story of 'The Three Billy Goats Gruff' was used, Colin lost eye contact because he laughed so much that he nearly unbalanced the chair. Laura recorded that since this intervention Colin used to say 'look at me' if members of his family did not respond quickly enough to his requests and he always looked directly at Laura when he wanted her to play or give him something.

14. Target behaviour

This intervention was initiated because Colin was not as relaxed as he could be for a child of his age. His gross as well as his fine motor movements were slightly uneven and jagged. The aim was to teach him to relax. Relaxation skills were viewed as a precursor to other behaviours such as play skills, academic skills, and the development of smooth gross and fine motor movement. Relaxation was defined as 'lying on the relaxation mat without fidgeting'. Once Colin was 'relaxed' the target was an increase in the duration for which he lay on the relaxation mat without fidgeting.

■ ■ ■ ■ ■ ■ ■ ■ ■ ■ ■ ■ ■ ■ □ □ □
1 2 3 4 5 6 7 8 9 10 11 12 13 14 15 16 17

PROCEDURE

Colin lay on a mat on the living room floor. Laura put a relaxation tape on and gently rubbed his arms or back. During the early trials, when Colin fidgeted or pulled away, Laura lay beside him and did 'really slow' exercises, such as stretching the arms and legs, pretending to swim slowly in the sunlight, or curling up like a snail, and told him to relax. Laura timed the duration of each trial.

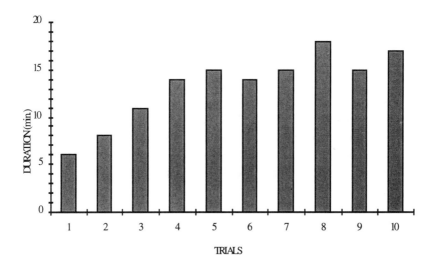

Figure 4.15 The duration with which Colin participated in relaxation exercises

RESULTS

Figure 4.15 shows the duration for which Colin relaxed during ten trials. Colin's ability to relax increased from 6 minutes during the first trial to a maximum of 18 minutes during Trial 8. The duration of Trials 9 and 10 was slightly shorter, but still over twice the duration of Trial 1. During Trial 1 Colin was fidgeting and pulling faces as Laura lay beside him and did 'really slow' exercises as described above. For the second trial although Colin fetched the mat himself, he was initially resistant and difficult to settle. Laura asked him to imagine being a sprouting 'seed', waving his 'leaves' while lying down. Then he was instructed to 'swim' slowly on his back. Laura then tried to rub his arms gently to relax him, but he fidgeted so much that she gave up

and rubbed his legs and feet gently instead. He gradually stopped resisting and lay back while Laura rubbed his arms and shoulders. After about eight minutes he said 'Put mat away' so Laura asked him for a hug and she asked him if he liked relaxing. He said 'Yep!' and put the mat away.

During the third relaxation trial in the living room Laura used massage oil. Colin was reluctant to participate. However, he allowed his feet and arms to be rubbed and Laura reported that there were moments of calm and relaxation. During the next session, again in the living room there were more prolonged periods of relaxation. Colin put the mat away after 14 minutes.

When Laura rewound the tape in preparation for the next session Colin heard snippets of the music and said 'relax' and 'get the mat'. He then went and got the mat and switched on the music. He was fidgety at first but soon curled up, then uncurled, moved like a tree and swayed while lying down. He relaxed for a much longer period. Because he refused to take off his socks and shoes, Laura rubbed oil on his arms and back. She commented that he 'will go floppy now when asked'. After this trial Laura and Colin were in a restaurant when Colin was leaping on his seat. Laura asked him to sit down and he complied saying 'relax'.

Trial 6 took place in the sitting room. Laura concentrated on Colin's hands and arms. She reported that there was less resistance, some real relaxation. There was a break in the tape and Colin made no attempt to get up. Trial 7 took place after Colin's bath. Laura said that he can now 'flop' on request and that he likes relaxing.

The next trial started with some resistance. Initially Colin put away his mat. However, eventually he settled on the mat. A new tape was put on and Colin had brief intervals of real relaxation while he chatted quietly about his day. The new tape was by the singer Enya. In the car that day Colin's sisters requested that a tape with very similar music was played over and over again. Colin fell asleep in the car. Laura commented that this was the first time this had happened in months.

Trial 9 began with resistance again, but there were short periods of stillness and relaxation. Colin's sister joined in the last trial. Colin was restless, but his sister almost fell asleep. However, Colin could 'go floppy' when asked.

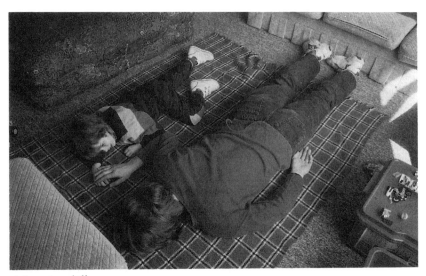

Relaxation skills

DISCUSSION

An intervention was designed to teach Colin relaxation skills and to increase the duration for which he was able to relax. During ten trials Colin learned to relax relatively deeply for an increasingly long duration.

It is difficult to define and measure relaxation. While most behaviours during Colin's treatment were open to observation by Laura or others, relaxation was not observable in the same sense. The only way Laura was able to gauge whether or not Colin was relaxing was to observe Colin's responses closely. Laura found that Colin fetched the mat himself and put it on the floor at the beginning of each session. He lay down willingly and made no attempt to leave the mat during most of the sessions. Furthermore, she found that Colin remained in the same position for a prolonged time without getting tense or fidgeting.

Relaxation is so difficult to define and measure because it is more about feelings and thoughts than anything else. Some people say that there is a great difference between feelings and thoughts and behaviours because feelings and thoughts cause behaviour. Behaviour analysts view this issue differently. They say that feelings and thoughts are behaviour. How come? First of all let's go back to the definition of behaviour used by behaviour analysts: Behaviour analysts say, *behaviour is anything people do*. Now let's look at feelings and thoughts again. Is it not true to say that people *do* feel, or that they *do* think, and that each of these activities occupies periods of time? Because feeling or thinking are things that people do, it makes sense for them to be categorised as behaviours. Once they are categorised as behaviour, though, new questions appear. For example, now that feelings and thoughts *are* classed as behaviours they cannot be said to *cause* behaviour; if they don't cause behaviour what does? Further, if feelings and thoughts *are* behaviour we need to find out what causes them as much as we need to find out what causes other kinds of behaviour.

We already know that behaviour analysts look for causes of behaviour in the environmental contingencies that prevail (see Chapter 1 and Chapter 3). In other words, behaviour analysts understand that behaviour is a function of environmental contingencies (i.e., the if–then relations between antecedents, behaviour, and consequences). In relation to feeling and thinking, behaviour analysts understand that not only publicly observable behaviours, but also private behaviours such as feeling and thinking are a function of contingencies (cf. Keenan, 1997). The example of Laura working on helping Colin to learn to relax gives a perfect illustration of how one may arrange contingencies to change private behaviours, in this case feeling relaxed and thinking relaxed thoughts.

The behavioural measure of relaxation for Colin was publicly observable: time spent on the relaxation mat without fidgeting. A variety of publicly observable measures can be used for interventions in which private behaviour is targeted. For example, when training assertiveness, the measure could be loudness of speech, when training 'caring for others', the measure could be latency with which a child turns to the other person when the other person starts to cry. The important point here is that not only can publicly observable behaviours be encouraged to develop, but private behaviours also can be changed by arranging appropriate contingencies.

15. Target behaviour

The educational psychologist had commented that Colin's '...failings in social awareness, social interaction and language development at present and their combination will make conventional classroom learning difficult'. Again we used this assessment to identify specific target behaviours that would have a bearing on how Colin would be viewed within the educational system, a system that was unable to advise Laura on specific steps to be taken to correct Colin's behaviours. Since Colin's parents wanted Colin to attend

■ ■ ■ ■ ■ ■ ■ ■ ■ ■ ■ ■ ■ ■ ■ □ □

1 2 3 4 5 6 7 8 9 10 11 12 13 14 15 16 17

mainstream primary school an intervention, known as the 'hiding game', was designed to target Colin's communication skills during peer play.

PROCEDURE

The procedure was carried out in the living room. The 'hiding game' was played by two players as follows: one person (the 'finder') had to leave the living room while the other person (the 'hider') hid sweets anywhere in the room, e.g., under the cushion on the settee, on top of the shelf, or behind the dresser. Colin chose which sweets were to be hidden, e.g., Smarties®, M&Ms®, and Skittles®. Using a tape recorder the 'hider' then recorded messages that helped the 'finder' to find the sweets, e.g., 'There are Smarties® under the cushion on the settee'. The 'finder' was then brought back into the living room to listen to the first message. When s/he found the sweet, s/he was allowed to eat them. The 'finder' then listened to the next instruction of where to find the next sweet, and so forth. Colin took turns in playing the part of 'finder' or 'hider', his sisters, brother, or father took the other part.

After the first time the game was played, small paper notes were hidden instead of sweets. Consecutive numbers were written on these notes and they had to be found in sequence before the final message indicated where the sweets were hidden. Throughout the time the game was played the number of hiding places increased from three to six.

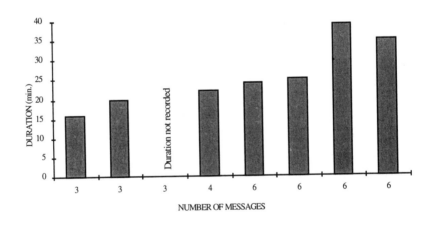

Figure 4.16 The duration with which Colin played the 'hiding game', receiving and leaving an increasing number of messages

■ ■ ■ ■ ■ ■ ■ ■ ■ ■ ■ ■ ■ ■ ■ □ □
1 2 3 4 5 6 7 8 9 10 11 12 13 14 15 16 17

RESULTS

Figure 4.16 shows the results achieved with the 'hiding game'.
With an increase in the number of messages (from 3 to 6) a steady increase in
the duration of the game was achieved (from 16 minutes to 39 minutes).

DISCUSSION

An intervention was designed to increase Colin's communication skills
during peer play. The 'hiding game' was played eight times. A steady increase
in the duration of the game was recorded. An increase in the complexity of
verbal communication was also observed, e.g., during Trial 7 Colin left
messages such as 'No. 1 is in the hall in the doll's house', or 'In a drawer, in the
sewing machine, left hand drawer'. In effect, Colin was helped to develop his
social awareness, social interaction, and language.

Laura recorded that the 'hiding game' was highly enjoyable and Colin got
very excited, so much so that the first time he played it he told his sister where
to find the sweets and then he ran and ate them himself. Laura commented
that Colin was reprimanded by his sister. Yet this did not detract from the fun
everybody had playing this game.

While the educational psychologist observed deficits in Colin's behaviour
that, if not treated, would leave Colin unprepared for mainstream education,
he did not recommend detailed procedures as to how this could be remedied.
The important point during this intervention was that behavioural deficits
can be treated and that this treatment can even turn into a family game.

16. Target behaviour

Role-play skills are usually viewed as an important part of play skills, since
they allow for behavioural rehearsal of otherwise difficult to train
behaviours. For example, children can learn a wide range of social skills such
as problem solving or appropriate peer interaction. This intervention focused
on introducing role-play to Colin's play skills. Duration of playtime as well as
complexity of role-play were assessed.

PROCEDURE

A doll's house was set up in the sitting room. Colin was seated in a small chair
facing Laura. There were four trials in which Laura told Colin a brief
children's story, e.g., 'Goldilocks' (used for two trials), 'The Three Little Pigs',
and a story created by Laura about three giants. During the story Laura
gradually turned Colin's chair round until he faced the doll's house. She then

prompted Colin to role-play the story using the dolls' house and the dolls, e.g., she said 'Let's see if mummy bear made some porridge'.

RESULTS

The duration of the trials ranged from 12, to 35, to 30 to 29 minutes. Initially Colin was prompted to role-play the story, but during Trials 2–4 he role-played the story without further prompts and accompanied his play with lots of chat.

DISCUSSION

An intervention was designed to introduce role-play to Colin's play skills. During four trials play time varied from 12 minutes to 35 minutes. An increase in the intensity of play was reported by Laura. On a number of occasions the sessions had to be terminated due to outside interference such as the need to collect other children from school or his brother coming in with another toy. This kind of interference was usually kept to a minimum during training trials with Colin. However, during this intervention playtime was often longer than half an hour and had become a natural part of family life.

17. Target behaviour

Colin had started school a month prior to this intervention. Colin's teacher reported that Colin was unwilling to sit – even when supervised – at a table and complete simple academic tasks. The aim of the following procedure was, therefore, to enable Colin to complete simple 'paper and pencil' tasks and to do this with decreasing levels of supervision.

PROCEDURE

Colin was seated at a table. A pencil and sheets of paper were placed on the table in front of him. He was instructed to complete simple 'paper and pencil' tasks, such as drawing a matchstick man, filling in missing letters, writing numbers 1–9, writing his name, copying letters of the alphabet, counting objects, finishing the house picture, circling 'the same'. When Colin stopped working, Laura used verbal instructions to prompt him to continue, such as 'Draw another leg on the man', 'Write the next number'. The intervention was carried out in eight sessions. During each session four trials were carried out, i.e., Colin was given four academic tasks to complete. The total number of trials was 32. During this intervention the duration of the interval between instructions was measured.

■ ■ ■ ■ ■ ■ ■ ■ ■ ■ ■ ■ ■ ■ ■ ■ ■
1 2 3 4 5 6 7 8 9 10 11 12 13 14 15 16 17

Once the data showed that the duration between instructions increased, in other words, that Colin was increasingly completing tasks on his own, the next procedure was introduced. Colin was again seated at the table and sheets of paper and a pencil placed in front of him. The tasks given to Colin were similar to those in the previous procedure. Initially Laura supervised Colin's work. The supervision was withdrawn in the latter part of the treatment. The duration of trials was measured.

RESULTS

Figures 4.17 and 4.18 show the results of these interventions. Figure 4.17 represents the increasing time span (duration) between instructions over eight sessions. Colin continued to work while Laura reduced the rate of instruction from one instruction every 29 seconds (Session 1) to one instruction in every 65 seconds (Session 8).

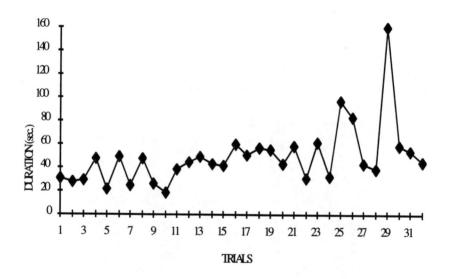

Figure 4.17 The duration with which Colin worked on academic table-top activities between instructions

The second part of this intervention (see Figure 4.18) was carried out for eight sessions (i.e., 32 trials) and resulted in an increase in time spent on academic task without supervision.

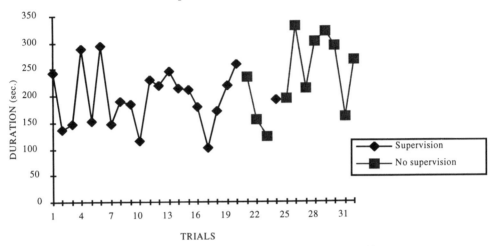

Figure 4.18 The duration with which Colin worked on academic table top activities with and without supervision

For the first five sessions (Trials 1–20) Colin was supervised. Colin worked between two and five minutes on each of these trials. During Sessions 6, 7 and 8 (Trials 21–32) he worked without supervision for between two and five-and-a-half minutes in each trial.

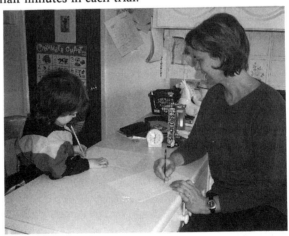

Academic skills

An intervention was designed to enable Colin to work on simple academic tasks with decreasing levels of supervision. Results show that this aim was achieved during two procedures over eight sessions each. The first procedure enabled Colin to work for an increasing duration without instruction. The second procedure enabled him to work increasingly without any kind of supervision.

The educational psychologist had identified what he called 'particular islets of ability' in Colin (i.e., identification of shapes; circle, square, triangle; name of primary colours, ability to count to 100 and ability to identify numbers, symbols and letters). This terminology and assessment had caused Laura much distress, as she had recognised that Colin had advanced skills in some areas. These skills were no different than those displayed by a typically developing child that is advanced for his/her age. For Colin's skills to be recognised as typical or even advanced, he also had to be able to sit and concentrate, work without supervision, and complete tasks with little or no supervision. This intervention laid the foundation for these skills.

General discussion

In this chapter we have described the careful application of well established behavioural principles in individualised programmes that were designed to bring out the best in Colin. At the end of the year he had made considerable progress and was attending mainstream primary school, supported by a teaching assistant 15 hours per week. By the time this book is published Colin will be seven years old. Laura has continued behaviour analytic work with him focusing on target behaviours that are much more elaborate and sophisticated than those we worked on in the early days. The many lessons learned during the first year of treatment can be summarised under the following headings;

(1) Changing the way you think about autism

(2) Selection of target behaviours

(3) Selection of procedures and data collection

(4) Selection of reinforcers

(5) Private behaviours

(6) Generalisation and maintenance

■ ■ ■ ■ ■ ■ ■ ■ ■ ■ ■ ■ ■ ■ ■ ■ ■

1 2 3 4 5 6 7 8 9 10 11 12 13 14 15 16 17

(1) Changing the way you think about autism

Before Laura was introduced to Behaviour Analysis, professionals in the field of autism had by-and-large advised her to accept Colin as he was and learn to live with his disability. They had told her that not a lot can be done before he enters school and that once at school the teachers would know how to handle Colin and he would be well looked after. Another one of the parents from PEAT put it like this: 'If your child cannot walk they offer you a buggy. Behaviour Analysis is different. If your child cannot walk, Behaviour Analysis shows you how you can try and teach him to walk.' This transition from the traditional approach to autism to a behaviour analytic approach was like an eye opener for Laura. Finally she had met with people who did not only offer 'tea and sympathy' but who offered a concrete approach to helping with everyday problems.

Behaviour Analysis does not promise a cure. Laura was conscious of this. However, Behaviour Analysis offers improvements. It does so by shifting the focus of carers to the application of established principles of behaviour and to the need for accountability in their implementation. Laura quickly found that many aspects of Colin's behaviour improved. It was hard work. Yet once the first improvements were achieved, such as increases in the quality of eye contact, decreases in stereotyped behaviours, and improvements in communication skills, Laura fully embraced the approach and made it her own. She soon developed her own individualised programmes for Colin. After all, she was the one who knew him best. She also had the experience of raising four older, typically developed, children, and their behaviour often provided yardsticks in helping to identify the areas in which Colin had not reached his full potential.

(2) Selection of target behaviours

One of the hall-marks of behaviour analytic treatment is that the aims of an intervention must be clearly stated and agreed by those involved in carrying out the treatment. In Colin's case this meant that prior to treatment a 'target behaviour' had to be identified, and clearly defined. Identifying target behaviours has to be a joint process between child (if possible), parents, and behaviour analysts. All three parties have an important role to play.

(i) The child, if possible, can help identify things he would like to be able to do. Realistically speaking, however, it is unlikely that a very young child will have a critical influence on choosing the target behaviour, for obvious reasons. This inability to give fully informed consent to procedures aimed at behaviour change is, however, not peculiar to Behaviour Analysis. Children do not usually give informed consent to be toilet trained, taught to speak, dress, behave in social situations, or eat with a knife and fork. These are culturally determined educational goals that are generally accepted by the society in which they evolved.

(ii) Parents have a very important part to play in the identification of target behaviours. They have the advantage of knowing the child and his/her environment intimately. They are in a good position to identify behavioural excesses and deficits, preferred activities, and reinforcers. Furthermore, they are the ones who will carry out the majority of the programme.

(iii) The role of behaviour analysts who work with parents is to impart theoretical knowledge and experience. They usually have the advantage of a certain level of emotional distance from the child. This enables them to view behavioural excesses and deficits more objectively. It is their job to ensure that target behaviours are clearly identified and properly defined.

Without full agreement between all participants regarding the 'target behaviour', an intervention cannot be implemented and treatment gains cannot be assessed. A guideline for what it means to have a clear definition is that everybody has to agree when asked, 'What would I need to see the child do in order to be able to say that he is now engaged in the target behaviour?' Take the example of eye contact. It is not enough to state simply that the target behaviour is eye contact. All too often target behaviours are loosely defined like this. This makes data collection incredibly difficult. To take another example, if the target behaviour is called 'attention', we don't know what we would need to see the child do in order to say that s/he is now paying attention. A clearer definition would be 'the child sits quietly on a chair and maintains eye contact until the parent finishes the instruction'. With this kind of definition a number of people could confidently agree on whether or not the child is in fact engaged in the target behaviour.

Another important aspect of identifying the target behaviour is that we need to be clear about what dimension of the target behaviour will be addressed during an intervention; is it the duration of eye contact (how long he is looking at me); is it the frequency (how often he is looking); or is it the latency (how quickly he is looking, after being called)? Once you have identified the dimension along which the target behaviour is to be measured, it cannot be changed during that particular intervention, otherwise the measurement is invalid. However, at times it becomes apparent during an intervention that more than one dimensions of a target behaviour should be addressed. In this case we need to implement an intervention to target each of the dimensions. We did this with regard to Colin's eye contact. First, we found that we needed to work on latency of eye contact (i.e., the time it took Colin to look up after his name was called), later we worked on duration (i.e., the length of time he was able to keep eye contact). Only when those who are concerned with the treatment are clear about what constitutes the target behaviour, and what measure they are using, can the data collected during the intervention become meaningful.

(3) Selection of procedures and data collection

After reading reports of successful procedures parents may be tempted to replicate these with their own child. At times this kind of replication may be successful. However, we should never forget that because each child is an individual a procedure that is successful with one child may not be successful with another unless it is adjusted to suit the child in question. Behaviour analysts do not prescribe procedures to be used with all children, instead they design individual programmes for individual children.

The need for individualising procedures becomes apparent when parents accept the pivotal role of data collection. The collection of data on an agreed dimension of a target behaviour is critically important. The main reason for this is that without data we cannot be confident that the intervention is actually working. There were times when the procedures identified for Colin did not achieve the desired results and we had to go back to the drawing broad and redesign aspects of the intervention. This was only possible because Laura continuously recorded the target behaviour throughout each treatment. Keeping accurate data allowed us to adjust procedures, basing our decisions on the data collected.

(4) Selection of reinforcers

A pre-requisite of any behaviour analytic intervention is the identification of effective reinforcers. As was described in Chapter 3, reinforcers are not defined by what they are but by what effect (or function) they have on the target behaviour. Initially, Colin only responded to edible reinforcers. That is why we used them. Yet, edible reinforcers, such as sweets etc., have a range of side effects. First, they are not too good for the child's health. Second, they are not always available; for example, you may not have them with you on a walk or in the car. You can therefore not use them when you are implementing an intervention ad hoc. Third, they are very obvious when used in public. Fourth, they are not commonly used with typically developing children. For these reasons we began to pair edible and social or activity reinforcers (i.e., use them at the same time) so that soon we were able to use only social or activity reinforcers, such as hugs and kisses, playtime with a favourite toy, and verbal praise, such as 'well done' and 'good boy'. These social or activity reinforcers are a more natural and common way of reinforcing a child's behaviour (any child's). Later Colin learned to respond to things like the 'fun in a game', or the 'beauty of a picture' he had drawn, or the 'sophistication of a bridge' he had built with his bricks. The progress from edible to social and activity reinforcers, to these natural reinforcers was something that was highly rewarding for all of us.

(5) Private behaviours

Much misunderstanding of Behaviour Analysis stems from the fact that by-and-large behaviour analysts start their intervention aimed at publicly observable behaviours. Critics of Behaviour Analysis then conclude that this is all behaviour analysts are interested in. This is clearly not the case. Behaviour Analysis is very much interested in private behaviours such as feelings and thoughts. For example, although in the main we concentrated on developing certain publicly observable behaviours with Colin we were aware that our interventions also had an effect on his private behaviours that would manifest in emotional, cognitive, attitudinal, or perceptual changes.

The big difference between behaviour analysts and non-behaviour analysts in relation to private behaviour is the way private behaviour is viewed and treated. Most non-behavioural professionals, such as social workers, educational psychologists, child psychiatrists, are trained within a tradition that interprets private behaviours as causes of public behaviours. In other words, they are trained to observe public behaviours, such as Colin drifting away from an activity, and then to make inferences about the cause of this by hypothesising about his private behaviours. Traditionally trained professionals would say that Colin is drifting because of his lack of concentration. Technically his private behaviours are viewed by these professionals as independent variables that *cause* his publicly observable behaviours, the dependent variables. Behaviour analysts view this differently. They say that Colin's public behaviours (i.e., drifting from an activity) as well as his private behaviours are both dependent variables that are related to each other, and that the nature of this relation is affected by interactions with the physical and social environment. This is a most important difference (cf. Keenan, 1997). Clearly the way we interpret the causes of behaviour will guide the way we plan treatment.

(6) Generalisation and maintenance

Treatment is not complete until the target behaviour has generalised and is maintained. This means change that is achieved during treatment should not only transfer to other situations or people (generalisation), but it should also outlast the intervention (maintenance). In order to achieve both general-isation and maintenance we have to include them in the treatment plan.

In Colin's case we included generalisation training by using other people, such as his father, his sisters, and their friends to carry out interventions that were similar to those carried out by Laura. Sometimes Laura herself carried out interventions in different situations, in the car, in the shop, in another room in the house. Interestingly, generalisation is an ability that once learned seems to 'generalise' itself. For example, once Colin was taught to make eye contact with other people and in other situations, he began to engage in behaviours that had not actually been included in generalisation training in new situations, e.g., he used his new language skills in the playgroup.

Regarding the maintenance of behaviour, there are a range of ways of ensuring that changes in behaviour are enduring. In most cases, behaviour analysts would implement what is known as a variable schedule of reinforcement. This means that rather than reinforcing the behaviour every time it occurs, reinforcement becomes less frequent, or unpredictable. If this is done carefully and correctly, the child will begin to work harder to gain a reinforcer even though it is delivered on an infrequent basis. Another way to ensure behaviour change lasts is to ensure that natural reinforcers take the place of arbitrary ones. We did this with Colin for a number of behaviours. For example, we planned for maintenance of eye contact, by making sure that he engaged in eye contact before he got anything he wanted during the normal run of the day, such as toys, drinks, and attention.

Conclusion

In this chapter we told you some of Colin's story during the first year of treatment. At the time of writing this was three years ago. After three years of behavioural intervention, you are probably asking: 'What is Colin like now?' Well, he's a talkative, happy and lively seven-year-old with a range of interests, a keen fan of Manchester United and Michael Schumacher (the racing driver), and he has a great sense of humour. He has a number of 'best' friends; he joins in the playground games and really enjoys football. When he grows up, he wants to be a Formula One driver or an Egyptologist – which doesn't sound so impressive once you know it's been inspired by an exciting episode of 'Goosebumps' on TV with a rampaging mummy.

In class, he's beginning to contribute to discussions without prompting which is a big change. His number work, reading and comprehension are all good and on a level with his peers. His reading is particularly good, above his age expectancy, and he chooses a wide range of books to read for enjoyment. Three years ago Colin was diagnosed with 'underlying learning difficulties'. ABA viewed these difficulties not as limitations but as challenges to the sophistication and precision that was required to teach him. He was also diagnosed as having 'isolated islets or splinters of ability', for example in symbol recognition. ABA viewed these abilities not as freak occurrences that 'proved that he was autistic', but as actual skills that could be built on.

A recent school report stated that '[Colin's] concentration and attention spans are really improving. He can listen well and volunteers comments in story/discussion. His reading and written expression are of a very high standard, as is his command of spelling'. Emphasis is now on encouraging social participation, and increasing his contribution in whole-class work. Even in this area of acknowledged difficulty, there is continuing progress.

Colin's social development has shown great improvement. He is now '...contributing in a meaningful way to a group activity in structured play. He likes to share 'news', toys etc. with friends, and his conversation skills are improving steadily'. Laura is still using Behaviour Analysis, working on areas of concern such as his fine motor skills (handwriting and colouring are not as good as they should be for a seven-year-old) and independence in self-help skills, such as getting dressed and getting ready for school. Looking at him objectively, Laura and Geoffrey can see there are still deficits, particularly in his social skills, but they see these now as challenges to be added to the list of behaviours they can analyse and probably change.

These improvements aren't miraculous, they are the result of a lot of intense, structured work, and they didn't happen overnight. Colin's parents needed the support and consistent approach of everyone involved in Colin's activities outside home as well:

'At the beginning we did not realise any of this would be possible. The "expert" opinion was that he would continue to have difficulty with language and learning, that he was of below "normal" intelligence (largely because his language was very delayed, and he scored so badly on standardised tests) and that his best opportunities lay in "special" education, miles from home with all the subsequent problems of isolation from the majority of children in the community. We realised this may not be the case for every child with autism, but it would be a welcomed change if the establishment (medical and educational) looked first for a child's potential, rather than concentrating on what the child is unable to do and project that into a future of "failing".

Looking back over the work we did, and the events of the past three years, the frightening thing is how much depended on chance. If our GP had not been interested in behavioural interventions (and how usual is that?), we would never have met Mickey and Karola, and we would never have had the opportunity to help Colin using ABA. I cannot imagine that Colin would be attending the same small school as the rest of the family – and fitting in so well – if he had followed the recommended 'education' for children with autism.

Other parents in our group will tell you about the difference between the behavioural approach and the "conventional" opinions about their children. Professionals and support groups involved with autism should at least bring this to the attention of parents, and let them decide if they want to find out more about ABA. The PEAT group was formed to share that information and teach the skills needed, though as a small organisation our resources are limited. Appropriate placements and support in nursery and school, whether "mainstream" or "special" are extremely important too – and as early as possible to maximise the effect of intervention. We realise that Colin was extremely lucky to have not only early behavioural intervention, but the encouragement of a very skilled speech therapist, who arrived in our area just as we began working with Mickey and Karola. The small rural school he attends, the energy, flexibility and patience of all the teaching staff, especially his wonderful teaching assistant, have undoubtedly been major positive factors in his subsequent development. For all of this, we're very thankful, but it shouldn't have been a matter of chance or a series of fortunate coincidences.'

References

Collins English Dictionary (3rd Edition) (1991) London: HarperCollins Publishers.

Dillenburger, K. and Keenan, M. (1995) Dealing with child problem behaviours effectively. *Child Care in Practice. Northern Ireland Journal of Multidisciplinary Child Care Practice, 1*, 33–38.

Dillenburger, K. and Keenan, M. (1997) Human development: A question of structure and function. In K. Dillenburger, M. O'Reilly and M. Keenan (eds) *Advances in Behaviour Analysis* Dublin: University College Dublin Press.

Keenan, M. (1997) W-ing: Teaching exercises for radical behaviourists. In K. Dillenburger, M.O'Reilly and M. Keenan (eds) (1997) *Advances in Behaviour Analysis.* Dublin: University College Dublin Press.

Keenan, M. and Dillenburger, K. (in press) *Behaviour Analysis. A Primer.* Multi-media tutorial. CD-ROM.

Masidlover, M. and Knowles, W. (1979) *Derbyshire Language Scheme.* Derby: Derbyshire County Council.

Pryor, K. (1984) *Don't Shoot the Dog. The New Art of Teaching and Training.* London: Bantam.

CHAPTER 5

What do we Want to Teach our Children?

Ken P. Kerr

In Chapter 4 some parts of the ABA programme of one particular child were described and discussed. This was done to give you an insight into the continuity of a programme and show you the attention to detail, commitment, and perseverance necessary to achieve progress. However, each child has a different learning pace and each programme is pitched at the individual child's level of skill. You will therefore find examples from different programmes with different children in this chapter. In order to retain an overview I will begin by introducing a general ABA curriculum and identify some of the main tasks that are commonly taught. The case examples in this chapter were chosen and reported by parents and are representative of the work undertaken by PEAT group members. The results are presented in a variety of different ways, including graphs depicting the minutiae of changes in behaviour, tables outlining long-term progress, and anecdotal reports. The aim is to show the level of refinement (and success) that parents and other carers can achieve by availing of structured courses on Behaviour Analysis.

Planning the curriculum

Autism is diagnosed when certain excesses and deficits are observed in a particular child's behaviour. It makes sense therefore that these observations should provide a starting point for designing a curriculum that suits the individual needs of each child. Once the starting point is identified the next task is to identify the direction of the teaching. The question is 'What do we want to teach our children?' This is a difficult question. Fundamentally, it is of course up to the parents to decide what they want to teach their children. After all it is the parents' right and responsibility to bring up, educate, and guide their child into adulthood. Practically, however, most parents are asking for help with these kinds of decisions when it comes to teaching their child with autism. ABA practitioners therefore have developed core curricula that ensure that basic pre-requisite skills are taught prior to complex skills. Figure 5.1 presents diagrammatically one such curriculum highlighting some of the main target behaviours within an ABA programme. It should be remembered, however, that this diagram is a template and that each curriculum needs to be tailored for the individual.

An overview of a general ABA programme

Figure 5.1 provides an overview of the main areas addressed in most ABA programmes. The overall aim is the development of life skills and self-management skills to allow the individual (and family) to experience the highest quality of life possible. The curriculum is broadly divided into three categories; learning readiness, academic skills, and play/vocational skills.

Learning readiness

Learning readiness refers to the kind of skills that are pre-requisite to the acquisition of more complex behaviours. During this phase the ABA programme is established with the child and it is therefore of vital importance that the child enjoys the programme and that a loving, caring relationship is established between the child and all the adults involved. By teaching learning readiness skills first, obstacles to further progress are removed. Learning readiness skills include basic compliance to simple instruction (e.g., 'sit down', 'point to …', 'give me …'), appropriate eye contact, and imitation. During this phase of the programme the majority of the teaching is conducted in one-step instructions followed by immediate reinforcement. Once these basic skills have been mastered, more complex tasks can be built into the programme.

Academic skills

Academic skills (including pre-academic skills) lie at the root of a wide range of educational and social activities that are necessary for independent living. They are therefore considered of major importance to any ABA programme. As with all ABA programmes the level of skill acquired will depend on the individual child, the timing of behavioural intervention, the intensity of the treatment, continuity between service providers, and parental involvement. The acquisition of academic skills involves the development of basic receptive and expressive language (i.e., understanding and communication skills), increasing the child's concentration span (i.e., the duration for which the child is able to engage with a task), the ability to work unsupervised, and the capability to complete tasks. During academic skills training instructions

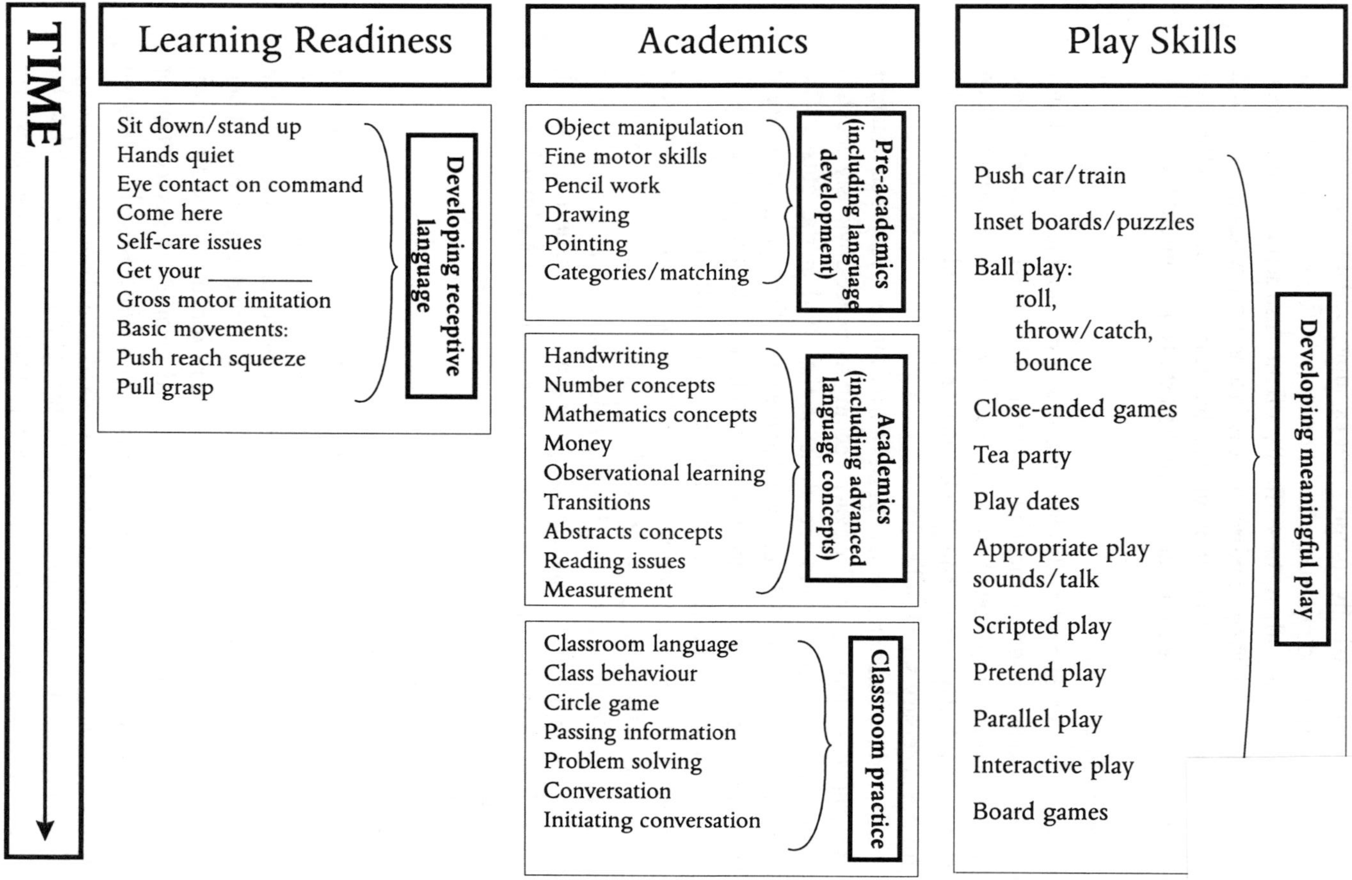

Play Skills

Developing meaningful play

Push car/train
Inset boards/puzzles
Ball play:
  roll,
  throw/catch,
  bounce
Close-ended games
Tea party
Play dates
Appropriate play sounds/talk
Scripted play
Pretend play
Parallel play
Interactive play
Board games

Academics

Pre-academics (including language development)

Object manipulation
Fine motor skills
Pencil work
Drawing
Pointing
Categories/matching

Academics (including advanced language concepts)

Handwriting
Number concepts
Mathematics concepts
Money
Observational learning
Transitions
Abstracts concepts
Reading issues
Measurement

Classroom practice

Classroom language
Class behaviour
Circle game
Passing information
Problem solving
Conversation
Initiating conversation

Learning Readiness

Developing receptive language

Sit down/stand up
Hands quiet
Eye contact on command
Come here
Self-care issues
Get your ___
Gross motor imitation
Basic movements:
Push reach squeeze
Pull grasp

TIME ⟶

Figure 5.1 Example curriculum areas in an ABA programme

usually become increasingly complex. For example, initially the child learns to respond correctly to two-step instructions (i.e., 'Lift the Teddy and put it on top of the table'), then the difficulty of the instruction is increased. Conditioned and delayed reinforcement is increasingly utilised. The child will learn tasks that are meaningful and functional, giving him/her the opportunity to engage in the newly acquired skills throughout the day.

Play and vocational skills

Play skills and vocational skills complement the development of academic skills. It is vitally important that children learn to be socially competent and able to interact appropriately with their peers. By progressing from isolated play, to parallel play, and meaningful interactive play, children can gradually learn the necessary social skills.

Each of these skills areas encompasses a wide range of very specific target behaviours (see Figure 5.1). The exact teaching sequence obviously depends on the individual needs and the skills of the child at the outset. The comprehensive nature of ABA ensures that the aims of any programme are in accord with the aims of the parents of that child and that the psychological, emotional, social, and intellectual needs of the child are met.

Given the individual nature of the treatment it is not surprising that families within the PEAT group are teaching their children at different levels within the curriculum. The following examples stem from these families and provide an insight into the therapeutic process and data collection. We will first look at some examples from programmes that are teaching learning readiness skills.

Learning readiness

Teaching Mason to make eye contact

Karen and Jon joined the PEAT group in May 1998. One of the first things they taught their son, Mason (age 3), was to make and maintain eye contact. Eye contact is a pre-requisite for academic skills and social integration. Karen and Jon decided to teach Mason that when he was given the instruction 'Look at me' he was to look at the instructor. They recorded any eye movement towards the teacher as a correct response, and recorded the percentage of correct responses, i.e., if Mason made eye contact six times when he was given ten instructions to look, they recorded this as 60% correct.

Initially Mason was to make eye contact for a period of one second, as his eye contact improved, the duration was expanded. Correct responses were reinforced with verbal praise. Sometimes, during the initial training prompts were needed, i.e., Karen or Jon gently guided Mason's head so that he was facing them. Gradually the amount of prompting was reduced and Mason turned his head and made eye contact on his own accord.

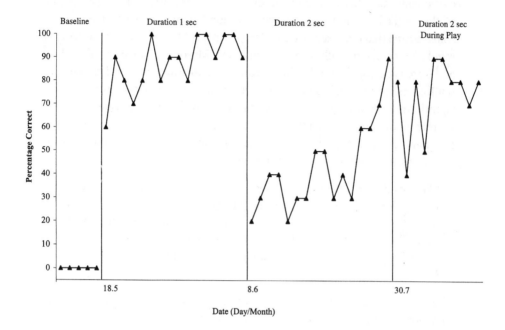

Figure 5.2 Results of an ABA programme to improve Mason's eye contact

Figure 5.2 shows that Mason made no correct responses during the baseline period. A substantial increase in the percentage of correct responses (making eye contact for one second following the instruction 'look at me') was noted during the first stage of the intervention. Given this data, Karen and Jon became optimistic and decided to increase the duration of eye contact required before Mason received verbal praise (i.e., reinforcement). Mason now only received verbal praise if he maintained eye contact for two seconds. Initially the percentage of correct responses decreased but the data shows that Mason gradually learned to keep eye contact for the longer period. In Phase 3, Karen and Jon decided to ensure that the newly acquired behaviour would generalise. For this purpose they used a play condition in which Mason was likely to be more easily distracted. The data shows that initially it was difficult for Mason to make the required eye contact, however, eventually his responses improved and averaged at a rate of 74% correct.

Bye-bye nappies

Karen and Jon also incorporated potty training into Mason's ABA curriculum. As with the teaching of eye contact, they first collected a baseline of the target behaviour; in this case the number of 'accidents' (i.e., wet or soiled pants) that occurred per day. They then got Mason to sit on the potty at regular intervals, initially every 15 minutes. Mason is a very sociable child and Karen and Jon found that he responded readily to cheers and clapping as reinforcers. Figure 5.3 shows that the result of this intervention was a significant decrease in the number of 'accidents' per day. Karen and Jon therefore decided to introduce a self-management element into the programme; when Mason needed to use the potty he was to lead one of his parents to the potty or ask for it. Karen noted:

> 'We stayed close to Mason and observed him as much as possible. When we positioned the potty Mason began to go over to it and sit down on it fully clothed. We would then help him to use the potty successfully. Mason began to take us by the hand and we taught him to say "potty". We saved "bigger" reinforcers for independent requests and this pleased Mason.'

The data presented in Figure 5.3 show that Mason was able to say 'bye-bye' to nappies about two weeks after the intervention had started.

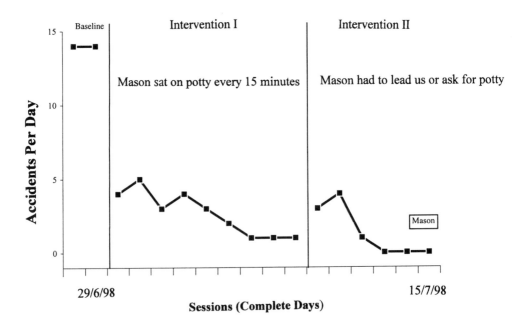

Figure 5.3 Results of an ABA programme to potty train Mason

Jack's tantrums after school

Jack is eight years old, and has been diagnosed as having a learning disorder with autistic tendencies. His parents, Hilary and John have been members of the PEAT group since it began. Hilary has already described one of the problems that interfered with normal family life in Chapter 1: Jack's temper tantrums after school in order to get Coke®. In this chapter Hilary and John report the data they collected with regard to this problem. Hilary noted:

> 'I was having problems with Jack when he returned home after school. He would shout for Coke®/ Pepsi® and would scream, jump and cry, until I gave in and he got his Coke®. I did an ABC chart for a few days and it was obvious that when he did not get Coke® on request, he would tantrum.'

As Hilary noted, the use of an ABC chart (see Chapter 3) to identify the variables that controlled the tantrum clearly illustrated the on-going pattern. Jack's tantrums functioned to access the desired object, Coke®. The procedure that Hilary and John devised with the help of their behaviour analyst was for Hilary to say 'No' when Jack requested Coke® and provide no further attention (i.e., reinforcement) if a tantrum occurred (i.e., put the tantrum on extinction). Verbal praise (i.e., 'good quiet Jack') was used if no tantrum occurred or when the tantrum stopped. In addition, Hilary used attention to positively reinforce any appropriate behaviours, such as Jack asking for Coke® in a suitable manner.

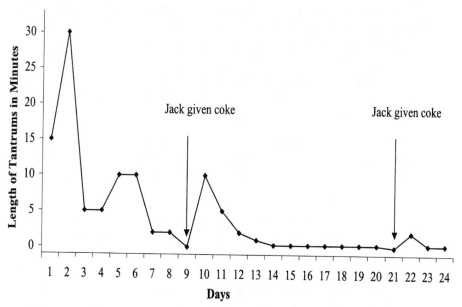

Figure 5.4 Results of an ABA programme to decrease Jack's tantrums wanting 'Coke'

Figure 5.4 shows the steady decrease in the duration of Jack's tantrums. Interestingly, following the two occasions on which Jack did receive Coke® the duration of his temper tantrums increased. Fortunately, Hilary collected data continuously and was therefore able to detect this increase immediately.

A second part of the programme (not recorded) involved the identification of other, more appropriate ways for Jack to obtain Coke®. Hilary noted:

> 'We also encouraged Jack to ask for things properly, he didn't get what he wanted if he did not ask properly, or even point quietly instead of shouting and screaming. In total the programme lasted 24 days. I was able to cope with the tantrums because I set up the environment, and I was in control of the situation not Jack.'

This example emphasises the importance of teaching the child skills that serve the same function as the original inappropriate behaviour. Assuming that the tantrums occurred to access Coke® it is important that Jack is able to access Coke® through a more functional (appropriate) means of communication.

Teaching Enda gross motor skills

Derek and Jean joined the PEAT group in February 1999. Following the implementation of a basic ABA curriculum they began to teach Enda (aged 4 years 9 months) gross motor imitation including clapping his hands, lifting his arms up, touching his cheeks or nose, putting his hands on his head, or tapping his belly. Imitation skills were identified as necessary precursors to more advanced movements. Initially they had taught him these skills using discrete trials to a criterion of 90% correct. Although they were pleased with his progress they realised that he did not engage in these behaviours smoothly or 'fluently'. His ABA teacher reported:

> 'Enda's parents had used a discrete trial training format. Discrete trial training, however, had slowed down teaching and placed a ceiling on performance. All he could do was score 100% correct. Time or speed of response was simply not an issue.'

It was decided to teach Enda to achieve fluency in these behaviours. Basically, Enda was taught not only to engage in the required gross motor behaviours correctly but to do so as many times as possible in a specified period of time. The basic reasoning was that if Enda could become 'fluent' on this task, and a wide variety of others, that he would be better equipped to retain and apply these behaviours in natural settings. Behaviour would then be seen to have a

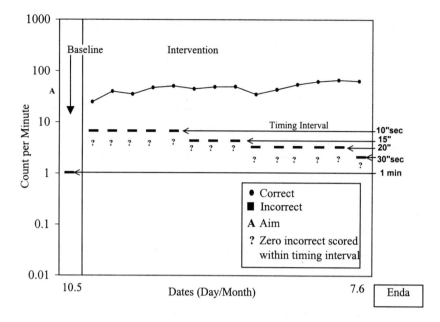

Figure 5.5. Fluency-based programme to teach gross motor skills

certain 'automaticity' or fluency commonly seen with experts in any field (Binder, 1996).

The baseline condition in Figure 5.5 shows that in one minute Enda scored ten correct and seven incorrect responses in the range of motor skills described above. These skills had been taught individually using discrete trials but Enda was clearly not fluent in the combination of these skills. The fluency based procedure consisted of setting an 'aim' by getting Enda's peers to engage in the same task. It was found that typical peers scored in the range of 40–50 movements per minute. Enda was taught to respond quickly by using a coaching technique whereby he was verbally encouraged to 'go quick', 'keep going', 'go faster'. A wide range of social and tangible reinforcers were made contingent upon his behaviour. Enda thoroughly enjoyed the 'quick fire pace' of the teaching situation. The effectiveness of this teaching was assessed within ten-second intervals. Enda's best score on the first teaching day was five correct responses and no incorrect responses in ten seconds. This was the equivalent of 30 correct responses and 0 incorrect responses per minute, which was slightly below the aim although considerably higher than the baseline. Once the aim was reached on three consecutive days the time interval was extended through 15 seconds, 20 seconds, to 30 seconds. Figure 5.5 shows that when the interval was increased to 30 seconds that Enda's correct response rate dropped slightly but soon recovered. Finally, he scored at a rate of 34 correct and 0 incorrect during a 30–second period, the equivalent of 68 correct and 0 incorrect responses per minute. The work is ongoing as it strives to ensure that Enda will retain and apply these skills over longer periods.

His ABA teacher reported:

'If you look at the data Enda was responding correctly 34 times in 30 seconds. It would have taken much longer to provide the same learning opportunities using discrete trials. Teaching to fluency involves both speed and accuracy. The result for Enda was more motivation, more enthusiasm, more enjoyment. A busy learner is a productive learner.'

Academic skills (Pre-academic skills)

Teaching Katie pointing

Katie was diagnosed as being autistic in July 1998 at the age of three years four months. Her parents, Stevie and Tina, joined the PEAT group in October 1998. Her parents noted:

'Katie was totally introverted. She had a blank canvas look and was unaware of anything going on in her environment. She had some play skills but these were mainly parallel skills whereby she would engage in an activity but still be totally isolated from her peers. She was independent in that she could access a lot of things she wanted, when she wanted. Her main means of communication was to push and pull us. This was difficult, as we often did not know what she wanted. She showed a lot of inappropriate behaviours the most troublesome were stripping, running, and pacing.'

After establishing learning readiness with Katie her home-based programme, targeted pre-academic skills, namely pointing. Stevie and Tina chose pointing as a functional skill because it would help Katie improve the quality of interaction at home. They decided that when they gave the instruction 'Point to _____', Katie should point to the object presented to her in the kitchen. Verbal praise was used as positive reinforcer. Katie's parents noted:

'When first teaching Katie to point we accepted an outstretched hand as a correct response. In this way Katie could easily experience success. Once she became proficient at this we began to use a hand-over-hand prompt to place her fingers gently into a pointing position. When we achieved this we would say "Good girl, this is pointing".
   We very quickly introduced "Point to bubble" as Katie loved bubbles. She appeared to like bursting the bubbles and it was therefore appropriate to use the bubbles to help produce fluent pointing. For each trial we blew a bubble and caught it on a little stick used to blow it, held it up, and said

"Point to bubble". Katie pointed to the bubble with her index finger outstretched and the bubble burst, which she thought was very funny. Praise was also given for doing this.'

Figure 5.6 shows that during the baseline Katie did not point to the object on request. During the intervention phase, when Katie's pointing was reinforced, a significant increase in pointing was noted. An average of 80% correct responding (i.e., pointing on request) was noted during this phase.

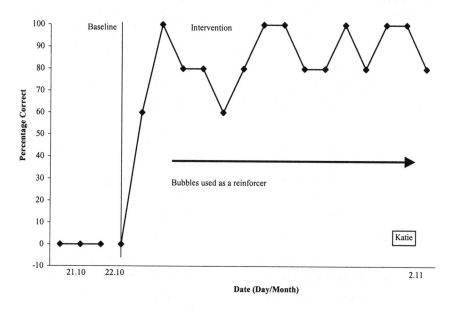

Figure 5.6 Results of an ABA programme to teach Katie 'Pointing'

The inclusion of baseline measures to record pre-intervention teaching was helpful. Having collected baseline data Stevie and Tina could be confident that their intervention was the cause of the increase in Katie's pointing. Stevie and Tina noted:

'We are delighted at how much progress Katie has made. She is beginning to use verbal communication. She will attempt to say "look" to gain our attention and will attempt to say "open" if she wants a door open. We realise that there is a long difficult road ahead. However, ABA has helped change our focus as well as help change Katie. We now are no longer afraid to tackle behaviour because it is considered to be typical of autistic children. Instead we concentrate on her excesses and deficits. We have learned that all behaviour is subject to the same influences. We hope to continue on with our home programme in conjunction with a school setting and are hopeful for continued changes in behaviour as Katie develops.'

Teaching Jack Big/Small

Hilary and John had difficulty teaching their son Jack the concept of 'big' and 'small'. They chose four items that Jack knew well; namely a car, a plate, a straw, and a dinosaur. Hilary placed pairs of big and small items on a table. She delivered the instruction 'Show me BIG dinosaur' (a similar procedure was used for 'small'; however, only the teaching of 'big' is presented here). If Jack did not respond correctly, she prompted him by taking his hand and reaching towards the target item and saying 'This is BIG dinosaur'. This was repeated for each item. As can be seen from Figure 5.7, the results of this procedure for the first three days showed a lot of variation. Based on the lack of consistent improvement in the data, Hilary and John decided to try a new technique. They noted:

> 'On the fourth day we started to use a very large box. When Jack was asked "show me Big Dinosaur" he had to put the Big Dinosaur in the Big Box. We also had a very small box, making sure it was small enough so the big items would not fit into it. By the fifth day Jack was getting 100% in all items. At one point we put Dad [John] in the Big Box and Jonathon [Jack's brother] in the small box. Jack found this part of the teaching hysterical.'

Figure 5.7 shows a clear improvement in the second phase of the programme where Jack was observed to have learned what 'big' meant. However, the lack of a clearly defined baseline makes the results difficult to interpret.

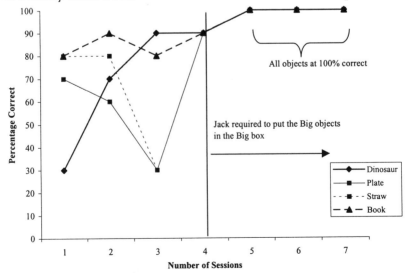

Figure 5.7 Results of an ABA programme to teach Jack 'Big'

Improving Kenneth's communication skills

Kenneth is nine years old. Although he exhibited certain unusual behaviours and difficulties ever since he was about two years old, the diagnosis of Asperger's Syndrome was not made until he was eight. This was partly because Kenneth also displayed exceptional academic behaviours that confused the picture. His mother, Brenda, began an ABA programme during March 1997. Using the skills she learned as a member of PEAT she has developed a highly creative programme which helps Kenneth in all walks of life. Brenda noted:

'The first thing I did was to carry out an "ABC" analysis (Antecedent – Behaviour – Consequence) on the behaviours that I considered to be in either excess or deficit. I focussed on behaviour under the following head-ings: social skills/communication, education, personal, management, co-operation, motor skills and ritualistic/self stimulation/displacement behaviours.

I made sure that Kenneth was aware that the ABA was a positive approach to learning. It was his behaviour that was inappropriate – not Kenneth as an individual. I was giving him the ability to acquire new skills. From the very start Kenneth enthusiastically accepted ABA both as a tool to help him learn things and as a fun challenge.'

Although Kenneth could speak, it was often very difficult to understand what he was saying. Brenda therefore decided to begin her work by improving Kenneth's communication skills. She noted that

'Kenneth is capable of speaking very well, but very often speaks unclearly or strangely, e.g., holding onto a syllable monotonously, mumbling quickly, or running all his words together so that even his close family cannot understand him. In social situations people often ask him to repeat himself. A typical response might be to refuse, mumble, or shout loudly, accusing the listener of not listening properly.'

Brenda devised a programme that became known as 'The Clear Speech Game'. The basic rules of the Clear Speech Game involved clearly defining instances of appropriate speech and inappropriate speech with particular focus on the following: volume, fluency, rate, clarity, intonation, manners, and grammar. All rules were explained and Kenneth was required to demonstrate correct and incorrect examples of rule following. The basic aim of the game as written by Brenda is as follows:

'Players should only speak when they are holding the beanbag. If you are not holding the beanbag you should listen carefully to the speaker. After the player has taken their turn at speaking, and there are no challenges, the beanbag is passed to the other player. As this happens, the player takes a counter from the middle and adds it to their pile. The winner is the person with the most counters after an agreed period of time.'

While one player was speaking, the other player listened carefully, and could challenge the speaker on the grounds that one or more of the clear speech rules was broken. Another ground for challenge was if a player spoke without holding the beanbag. To challenge, the listening played called 'Check!' and removed one of the opponent's counters and placed it on top of his or her own pile.

The baseline taken before the Clear Speech Game was implemented (Figure 5.8), shows that the number of instances of unintelligible speech (average 19.75) clearly outweighed the instances of intelligible speech (average 6.75). During the intervention of the Clear Speech Game the average number of instances of clear speech was 38.87 and the average instance of unintelligible speech was 1.87.

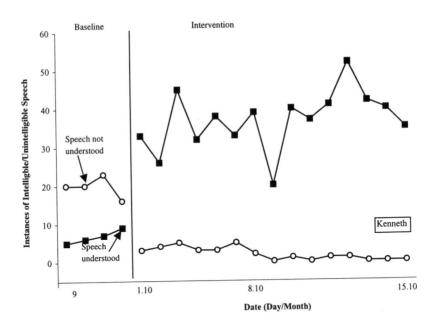

Figure 5.8 Results of using the Clear Speech Game with Kenneth

Teaching Kenneth to complete maths problems

One behaviour Kenneth would not engage in was completion of maths problems, despite the fact that standardised testing had ascertained that Kenneth was able to complete these problems. Brenda, in conjunction with a behaviour analyst, decided to use a token economy, a system where the individual earns access to favourite reinforcers for engaging in the target behaviour. A special ABA cupboard that contained Kenneth's ABA 'prizes' (i.e. toys, novelties, books, and sweets) was created in the house. Kenneth helped to design a price list, which set out the cost of accessing each reinforcer. Kenneth earned tokens for engaging in certain behaviours with more tokens earned for more difficult behaviour.

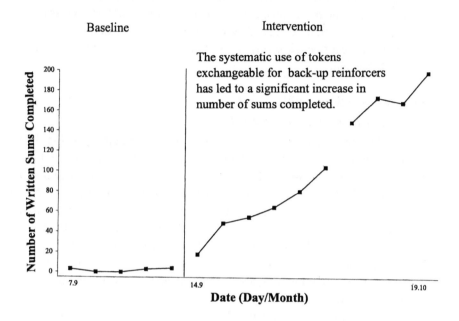

Figure 5.9 Results of an ABA programme to increase the number of sums completed by Kenneth

The baseline from Figure 5.9 shows an average completion of two sums per day. When the token economy was introduced so that Kenneth could earn certain consequences for completion of Maths problems he completed on average 106 problems per day. Kenneth now thoroughly enjoys completing his Maths and is keen to show how quickly and accurately he can work through the problems. His mother recently noted that his self-esteem seems to have increased along with his general confidence, and that his anxiety levels seem to have fallen. Finally, Brenda offers an insight into the importance of ABA for both Kenneth and herself:

'It has also helped me a lot in growing to understand and accept him while managing the difficult behavioural issues. Kenneth is now a keen ABA "fan" and has been closely involved in the design of many of the programmes. For Kenneth ABA is probably best described as FUN!

One year on I would say that ABA has been an extremely effective tool in helping Kenneth. We have seen significant improvements in many important areas such as clear speech, general compliance, eating, swimming, tying shoelaces, and handwriting. It has to be emphasised also that ABA is extremely hard work, but it is very worthwhile. I have heard it said that one of the reasons that ABA is attractive to parents is that it empowers them to help their children. In my opinion, ABA empowers the child with the skills so that they can help themselves develop. It is a healthy thing for people of any age to learn to take responsibility for their own behaviour.'

Play and vocational skills

Teaching Matthew independent play skills

Alan and Barbara have been PEAT members since the group began. Matthew (4 years and 6 months) attends school part time (3 hours per day) and gets 20–25 hours of one-to-one ABA therapy a week. One task that they taught Matthew was how to engage in independent play skills. By utilising a procedure with a clear starting point and a clear end point they taught Matthew to access a toy from a shelf, play with it appropriately, and to return the toy to its original position on completion of the play tasks. One of the main aims of this procedure was to teach Matthew a high level of independence so that he could access toys and activities when the therapists were not present.

The first step involved teaching Matthew the necessary skills required to complete the play task (e.g., threading buttons) at the table. It was necessary to ensure that Matthew could complete the activity unaided. Alan and Barbara chose tasks that Matthew enjoyed including matching, threading buttons and sorting a cutlery tray.

Once Mathew had mastered the chosen play activities, the second phase of the programme, namely teaching Matthew the play sequence, began. At first, Matthew was prompted through the sequence as required. For example, he was sometimes led to the toy shelf, or guided towards a play activity or back to the table, or prompted to play appropriately and then tidy the game away. By using prompting Matthew was easily able to experience success and gain access to reinforcers. The person giving the prompt stood behind Matthew and guided him gently without speaking. This method provided the least distraction possible and allowed the prompts to be more discretely removed.

The third phase of the programme involved teaching Matthew to choose a specific toy from the shelf. This procedure involved teaching Matthew to take a symbol and match it to the corresponding symbol attached to a box on the shelf. He then had to take the box to the floor and complete the activity before returning the box to the shelf.

Table 5.1 Mathew's progress on an ABA programme to teach independent play skills									
Date	Name of Tutor	Game	Match Symbol	Take Box to Floor	Take Game Out	Play Game	Put Pieces Away	Put Game in Box	Return Game to Shelf
17.9	Mum	Crazy Carrot	P	P	P	P	P	P	P
18.9	CS	Pennies	P	✓	✓	✓	P	✓	✓
19.9	CS	Crazy Carrot	✓	✓	✓	✓	✓	✓	✓
20.9	Mum	Crazy Carrot	✓	P	P	P	P	P	P
21.9	V.I	Crazy Carrot	P	P	✓	✓	✓	P	P
21.9	CS	Coins	✓	P	✓	✓	✓	P	P
21.9	CS	Crazy Carrot	✓	P	✓	✓	✓	✓	P
22.9	Mum	Crazy Carrot	✓	✓	✓	✓	✓	✓	✓
22.9	Dad	Crazy Carrot	✓	✓	✓	✓	P	P	✓
23.9	CS	Coins	✓	P	✓	✓	P	P	P
24.9	Dad	Coins	✓	P	✓	✓	✓	P	P
25.9	Mum	Tray	✓	✓	✓	✓	✓	P	
3.10		Buttons	✓	✓	✓	P	P	P	P
4.10	CS	Tray	✓	✓	✓	✓	P	P	✓
4.10	CS	Shoes	✓	✓	✓	✓	✓	✓	✓
4.10	CS	Tray	✓	✓	✓	✓	✓	✓	✓

P = prompt was used
✓ = independent responding.

A final phase of the programme involved increasing the number of play activities that Matthew was required to complete during a teaching session. After Matthew had mastered the completion of one play sequence (involving one play activity) per teaching session, Alan and Barbara gradually extended this to include four play sequences (involving 4 separate play activities) per session. Matthew now regularly completes a four-part sequence as part of a session and really enjoys it. Table 5.1 shows Matthew's success at the various stages of the sequence over time.

Case example: Chris

The following case history provides another example of how a carefully structured ABA programme can result in improvements in a variety of cognitive and social skills over a short space of time.

Chris was diagnosed in September 1997 at the age of two years nine months. Before this he was a placid boy with only occasional behavioural outbursts. His language skills were non-existent and he had no eye contact. Chris would not walk anywhere and had to be pushed everywhere in his buggy. He feared shopping centres with large crowds of people. His choice of food was very limited and he would refuse to eat his meal if presented with something new.

Five professionals assessed Chris over one day and diagnosed him as being autistic with a mental age of 12 months and a physical skills age of 18 months. Table 5.2 presents the scores from a variety of sub-scales including gross motor skills, personal/social skills, hearing and speech, and eye and hand co-ordination that were gathered as part of Chris's assessment. Comments from the senior clinical medical officer, September 4th 1997, reflect the poor scores that Chris had achieved on the variety of sub-scales:

> 'Christopher's performance in the Griffiths' revealed a somewhat patchy profile very much in keeping with the diagnosis of autism. It was noted through the developmental assessment that he had little, if any eye contact and when playing with a car he tended to upend it and spent a lot of time spinning the wheels of the cars around. It is clear that Christopher has delays across all areas of development which would be most marked in the area of his speech and language development. Performance skills and gross motor skills are also less than would be expected for a boy of two years and almost nine months.'

A report in September 1997 from the senior clinical medical officer, clinical psychologist and speech and language therapist also noted that Chris displayed poor eye contact, a lack of meaningful communication, he displayed no signs of symbolic play or joint referencing, and engaged in a few stereotypical movements. Interestingly, the report included a statement that 'the disability is lifelong although there is a tendency to improve with time provided there is appropriate education'.

At this point Peter and Hilary investigated the options of this 'appropriate education'. In October 1997, a friend told them of the PEAT group. After attending a workshop they set about establishing an ABA home-based programme for Chris. Peter and Hilary have been engaged in a home programme for approximately two years (1997–1999). They have focussed on the areas listed in the original assessment and have taught skills in a variety of areas. A summary of a report of an assessment on 16th June 1998 by the same senior medical officer as quoted above shows the progress that had been made in just nine months:

'I was absolutely delighted with his [Chris's] progress and whilst his assessment was not complete I would like to share with you the progress that he has made. In September of last year Chris's mental age equivalent of speech and language development was calculated at approximately 12 months and nine months later I have managed to score him at least at a 34 month level ... Similarly his performance skills which included jigsaws, etc. placed him at the 19.5 month level in September and he is now doing things at least at a 46 month level. Obviously this progress has been immense and must be attributed to (1) your intensive and dedicated input at home [on-going ABA programme], (2) attendance at Humpty Dumpty [Nursery], and (3) the support of a speech and language therapist.'

Chris was re-assessed on the areas above at the age of three years six months. It was found that he now had a developmental age of three years ten months. These are remarkable gains and bear testament to the efficacy of the teaching methods and the effectiveness of Peter and Hilary as teachers. After almost 18 months the picture of Chris has totally changed. His parents noted:

'The changes in Chris are nothing short of a miracle. He speaks in sentences, his eye contact is excellent, and the change in behaviour is immense. He loves to play board games like snakes and ladders and quite happily plays them with friends and family alike. He is fully toilet trained and the buggy is thankfully gathering dust in the garage.

He is currently attending a nursery school and is keeping up well with his peers. We have recently received notification from the education board that after all their recent assessments they recommend that Chris should enter into mainstream school: something 18 months ago nobody thought possible. His recent assessments show that his mental age and physical skills are age appropriate and although there remains work to be done with some social and pragmatic difficulties the board of professionals are so much amazed that the Senior Clinical Medical Officer has asked to use Chris as a case example for other professionals and for parents just receiving the diagnosis.

For us personally, the progress has been immense and to see Chris starting to develop his own sense of humour and for him to report his day's activities fills us with hope for the future.'

Table 5.2 Profile for Chris before and after implementation of an ABA programme			
Area	**Mental Age** *September 1997*	**Comments**	**Mental Age** *June 1998*
GROSS MOTOR SKILLS	21.5 mths	Christopher passed all Year 1 items, 19 out of 24 Year 2 items. He did not pass any Year 3 items.	40–51 mths
PERSONA/ SOCIAL SKILLS	18.5 mths	Christopher passed 13 items out of 24 in Year 2. He did not pass any items in Year 3. Results in this area were noted as 'quite patchy'.	Not given
HEARING & SPEECH	12 mths	Christopher was noted to engage in long babbled monologues. He passed a total of 19 items in Year 1. However, on assessment in Year 2, he only scored 5 out of a possible 24 items.	34 mths
EYE & HAND CO-ORDINATION	12 mths	Christopher passed the first 6 items of Year 2. He was noted to enjoy rolling the ball back and forth and scribbling straight lines on paper. There was no evidence of circular scribble, even during imitation.	54–57 mths
COGNITIVE PERFORMANCE	19.5 mths	It was assumed that he passed all items up including the end of Year 1 by following the rules of the Griffiths Assessment. He also passed 15 out of 24 items in Year 2.	46 mths

Summary

This chapter has provided an insight into the contents of an ABA programme. Initially the focus is on preparing the individual for the education process followed by teaching academic, social, and play skills. Once the child is taught learning readiness more complex behaviours from pre-academics, academics, play/vocational skills, and communication development can be taught. Examples provided throughout the chapter show the comprehensiveness of the programmes as well as how they can be tailored to suit the needs of the individual on any task. Different types of data have been presented along with observations by parents, all of which show the success of the teaching programmes. It is important to reiterate the importance of data collection as it allows the accurate assessment of each programme's success. Indeed, parents have come to realise the importance of keeping thorough data recording systems that then guide the future design of their programmes. It is fitting to conclude this chapter with a reminder of how learning behavioural principles can help parents change the focus of their understanding of autism. As Tina noted 'We now are no longer afraid to tackle behaviour because it is considered to be typical of autistic children. Instead we concentrate on her [Katie's] excesses and deficits.'

References

Binder, C. (1996) Behavioral fluency: Evolution of a new paradigm. *The Behavior Analyst, 19*, 163–197.

CHAPTER 6

Conclusion and Way Ahead

Mickey Keenan, Ken P. Kerr
and Karola Dillenburger

Introduction

It is often said that you can not be a prophet in your own country. For those of us who have struggled against the tide to teach Behaviour Analysis in university settings in Northern Ireland we are only too aware of this painful truth. This book, however, shows why it is important that we continue in our efforts to bring Behaviour Analysis to the community. It shows what can be achieved when parents and professionals together overcome obstacles that have prevented the tried and tested scientific advances of Behaviour Analysis from being shared with the people who would benefit from them most. Parents who contributed to this book are to be congratulated for their monumental effort in focusing their frustration, and at times despair, in reshaping a landscape that should have been prepared for them by properly informed professionals in the caring services. Parenting in itself can be a daunting task at the best of times. But our heart goes out to those parents who unexpectedly found themselves as students of a science of behaviour, applying their new knowledge to helping their children, and at the same time finding the energy to help to set up a new charity so that others also could benefit.

As a group we have made remarkable progress in a short period of time despite sniping from the sidelines by some who either were indifferent to our successes or who questioned the need for the group to exist in the first place. We still have a long way to go to achieve our ultimate aim of opening a school where all staff members are trained in Behaviour Analysis and where their collective skills can open up new avenues for all children with autism as well as to much needed research. Until then parents in the group will continue to perfect their skills in designing treatment plans and share their new-found knowledge and skills with other parents who hear about their successes.

Throughout this book we have shown that there is ample evidence for the effectiveness of Behaviour Analysis and that parents can be trained to be therapists. These findings, however, have not permeated all professional circles. This chapter concludes the book by emphasising the child's right to scientifically validated and effective treatment. We also point to some problems that parents may encounter should they decide to pursue training in a science of behaviour.

The child's right to effective treatment

In this book we have shown you what behaviour analysts mean when they say that your child has a right to scientifically validated effective treatment (cf. Van Houten, Axelrod, Bailey, Favell, Foxx, Iwata and Lovaas, 1987). We have shown you that the only way to do this is by collecting data prior to, during, and after treatment. All that remains to say here is that if you are unsure if your child is receiving effective treatment, be it in school, pre-school, from psychological services, or elsewhere, you should demand to see the data. This way you will be in a position to decide for yourself if your child is receiving effective treatment. Don't be surprised, though, if you encounter baffled faces with your request to see the data. Data taking is not as common as it should be and you may well find those in charge of the treatment programme of your child unable to provide you with data. The reason why data based decision making is not routinely implemented is that appropriate training in a natural science of behaviour is not widely available. This lack of training has lead to a range of misconceptions about what Behaviour Analysis is and what it does.

Prejudice and misconceptions

Almost all of you who are committed to a scientific approach to the treatment of your child will at some stage come across poor levels of support from those traditionally in charge of the caring services. The parents in the PEAT group repeatedly experience this lack of support. Lack of support is due mainly to lack of behaviour analytic training, which in turn has lead to superficial understanding and misinformation. Parents committed to Behaviour Analysis may encounter prejudice from other parents, from the medical profession, from educational psychologists, from clinical psychologists, from psychiatrists, from social workers, from professionals already trained in the treatment of autism by methods other than ABA. Examples of these misconceptions and their corrections are presented in Table 6.1.

Table 6.1 Misconceptions – and corrections – about Behaviour Analysis

Misconceptions	Corrections
Behaviour Analysis is simplistic and its practitioners simply follow recipes.	Behaviour Analysis is a sophisticated discipline that adopts a holistic approach to the study of behaviour. Its success in uncovering fundamental principles should not be confused with the apparent simplicity of these principles. Behaviour Analysis is constantly expanding as evidenced by its successful application to an ever broadening field of complex behaviours. Check these two Web sites for more information: 1. Association for Behavior Analysis: http://www.wmich.edu/aba/ 2. Cambridge Center for Behavioral Studies: http://www.behavior.org/
Behaviour Analysis does not deal with the underlying cause of a problem but deals only with symptoms.	Behaviour Analysis goes to the root of a problem, discovering and analysing the psychological principles that underlie what people do.
Behaviour Analysis is only interested in very simple, basic behaviours, not in cognition or emotions.	Behaviour Analysis offers an alternative interpretation of cognition and emotions as private behaviour. Research in this area is constantly expanding (cf. Keenan, 1997).
Behaviour Analysis is only applicable to severe behaviour problems.	If it works for severe behavioural problems, why not use it before things get that bad?
Behaviour analysts think of children as machines and their procedures treat them in a mechanical way.	Behaviour analysts are parents, sons and daughters, grandparents, aunts and uncles themselves who love their children just as much as anyone else. Confusing the precision required in the design of treatments with a mechanical outlook is like dismissing musical script as uninspiring when you haven't learned how to read it.
The ethics of Behaviour Analysis are problematic because it is manipulative.	However a parent or guardian interacts with a child there will be consequences. Critics somehow seem to be saying that developing awareness of the effects of these consequences is not to be desired.
Behaviour analysts do not give clients a say.	It is next to impossible to apply a good behaviour analytic programme without full co-operation.
Lovaas therapy is different from ABA.	O.I. Lovaas is a behaviour analyst who pioneered ABA with children with autism in UCLA in the 1960s and 1970s. He developed some ABA procedures that are highly effective. These are the procedures that are often referred to as Lovaas therapy.

On the whole, the erroneous argument often made is that Applied Behaviour Analysis is a cold science and that other treatment options offer a more empathetic approach to autism. Indeed it is common to find this view blatantly expressed as a concern about the ethics of ever using Behaviour Analysis (see a recent report by Jordan, Jones and Murray, 1998). To correct this inaccuracy you need to remember that Behaviour Analysis is about discovering and applying principles of behaviour not about promoting an ideology. Principles of behaviour are statements that describe the facts about how behaviour changes under certain conditions. If you exercise, your heart beats faster. That is a behavioural principle. It is simply a statement that informs us about the conditions that lead us to behave in the way we do. In a similar vein, the likelihood that other kinds of behaviour will occur is determined by a number of interrelated factors. At the simplest level, if you observe an increase in behaviour after it has been followed by some event, then we describe that change in behaviour as an example of the principle of reinforcement. If you try to produce an increase in behaviour and are unsuccessful, then you have to question your procedure and not the principle of behaviour. After all, would you agree with someone who said that it is impossible to make the heart beat faster? Presumably you would not! Probably you would query the procedures used to try to make it beat faster.

The translation of this natural science approach into procedures for changing the behaviour of a child with autism raises a problem for those who, for ideological reasons, promote the view that autism should be accepted rather then challenged or changed (cf. Schopler and Olley, 1982). However, those who question an effective approach to behavioural change should be made to answer this question: 'What is more accepting of a child than helping him to make the best of his life, to bring out the best in him?' This is a question that applies also to all aspects of parenting:

> 'After all, it is not a matter of whether parents will use behaviour-modification techniques to manipulate their children, but rather whether they will use these techniques unconsciously with unknown, unchosen and unhappy results, or use them consciously, efficiently and consistently to develop the qualities of their children.' (Hawkins, 1972)

Not all non-behavioural professionals are openly prejudiced against Behaviour Analysis. Indeed you may find some professionals saying that they are sympathetic to Behaviour Analysis but that they prefer an eclectic approach. Your first point of departure is to question their understanding of Behaviour Analysis. Where did they get their training? What recent behavioural journal articles have they read? Understanding a science that uncovers principles of behaviour is like understanding a science that uncovers laws of nature like gravity. It doesn't make sense to say you are sympathetic to a science that studies gravity, or that you prefer an eclectic approach. Gravity is gravity! It is a natural phenomenon, just like reinforcement or any of the other principles of behaviour that behaviour analysts have uncovered. Other professionals may say that they have tried behaviour modification and it did not work. This is a rather pessimistic conclusion based again on lack of training (cf. Walsh, 1997). Behavioural principles are always in operation, again just like gravity. If an intervention did not achieve the desired outcome the procedure should be changed; the fault is located in the procedure not in the behavioural principle. The reverse, of course, is also true where it is claimed that procedures have been devised that operate without the need for principles of behaviour (e.g., music therapy, play therapy, dolphin therapy, etc.). It is impossible to interact with the world without invoking behavioural principles. The task at hand for behavioural scientists is to collate these principles and to adapt them where possible to the needs of the individual or community. Evidence of effectiveness is all that is required.

Training in Behaviour Analysis

As with any form of prejudice, negative reactions to ABA stem from ignorance and, in the case of professionals, from a culture of misinformation that pervades much of the teaching in psychology and social work courses. The problem is so bad that members of the Association for Behavior Analysis have developed a Web site devoted to tackling examples of misrepresentation in general psychology text books and elsewhere. The site is called BALANCE and it is located at the following address: http://www.onlearn.com/balance.html.

The answer to why this state of affairs exists has more to do with the politics of ideology than with decision-making based on proven effectiveness. This conflict extends beyond the area of autism. At a recent meeting of the Experimental Analysis of Behaviour Group in London (April, 1998) Dr Mecca Chiesa from the University of Paisley in Scotland highlighted the stark reality of the problem. In her review of academic literature concerned with the treatment of a wide range of clinical problems she found that data showing Applied Behaviour Analysis to be more effective than other therapies were consistently ignored or misrepresented. At a more local level, students on the only course in clinical psychology taught in Northern Ireland barely get an introduction to Applied Behaviour Analysis despite its proven success in areas that fall within the purview of clinical practice.

Should parents be concerned with what looks like an argument between academics? Yes, very concerned! The people who hold the purse strings, or who run schools where staff are not trained in Applied Behaviour Analysis, are the people who manage the opportunities children have to develop. If these people are not educated about how to harness the principles of behaviour to facilitate development then the children will be short-changed.

The biggest issue, then, for parents who commit themselves to teaching their child is to find a person trained in Behaviour Analysis. It is not uncommon to find that some parents in the UK and Ireland have felt compelled into flying a behaviour analyst over from America or elsewhere to assess their child and to set up home programmes for them. While this may get them started, in the long run it can be problematic. Most important, it can have deleterious effects on the development of a programme that evolves with the progress of the child. This is because the behaviour analyst is not on hand to make crucial decisions at short notice if a particular programme needs adjusting because it is not having the intended effect. Fundamental questions like 'What should I do next?' essentially are put on hold until the next visit. This also can happen even when a particular programme is working. Of course some problems that arise in the course of therapy can be addressed in the short term by consultations over the phone, but only if you can afford it! To leave parents in such a vulnerable position is morally indefensible. As more and more parents become properly informed about ABA the problems for local service providers in the UK will be compounded. At some point in time they will have to acknowledge the findings of ABA and build up their own reservoir of suitably qualified therapists. This can take a long time if existing local resources are not fully harnessed and nurtured. Also, people brought in from outside a community are not really in a position to develop an appropriate infrastructure within that community. Understandably those who belong to profit making organisations might not even want to get involved because it would result in the depletion of a lucrative market for them.

What should you do? First, you should try to find out if there are behaviour analysts in your local area. While not all behaviour analysts are specialists in working with children with autism, they all understand and use the basic principles of behaviour. A local behaviour analyst will be able to help with the work aimed at decreasing behavioural excesses and increasing behavioural deficits, regardless of the kind of behaviours in question.

Second, you should try and find the right school for your child. Through behaviour analytic training sessions many parents have acquired more behaviour analytic skills than the professionals paid to look after their children. Schools that are forward looking will be open to sharing skills with parents and they will provide the best atmosphere for applying behavioural principles that facilitate the transition to school. Where a school is not helpful for children already in attendance, and believe it or not this does occur, any behaviour analytic training that the parents receive can be of tremendous help. For example, parents can make perfectly sensible demands regarding the collection of data by the school. Every scientist knows that data collection provides the yardstick for accountability. If specific procedures are implemented in a school for the benefit of a child, then it makes sense to have data collected on a daily basis to assess the efficacy of those procedures. This is what behaviour analytically trained parents do. It is reasonable, therefore, to expect professionals in a school to be equally scientific in their outlook. Data collected by a school will not only provide evidence that specific procedures promote development in a child, but will ensure also co-ordination of treatments between home and school.

Third, bearing in mind the general lack of formalised courses in Behaviour Analysis throughout the UK and the rest of Europe (though this is beginning to change), be sure you remain vigilant when someone says that they are familiar with Applied Behaviour Analysis. As yet there is no register of qualified behaviour analysts. In conversation you will be able to determine the extent to which they are familiar with basic issues such as, for example, the definition of behaviour used by behaviour analysts. Behaviour analysts view anything a person does as behaviour. Since people *do* think and *do* feel, cognitions and emotions are defined as behaviours, allbeit private behaviours, private for the individual in question.

This issue of the definition of behaviour is raised because all too often in statementing reports by educational psychologists you will see the term 'behaviour' treated separately from other categories such as cognitive skills and emotional development. Many of these professionals have been taught to pigeon-hole Behaviour Analysis as a collection of methods used for dealing with overtly disruptive or aggressive behaviour, and nothing more. Their training leaves them with the view that the psychology of a person is related to, but different from, the behaviour of that person. This shallow understanding of Behaviour Analysis finds expression in many books on autism not written by behaviour analysts. It is common, for example, to find isolated chapters that reference some of the principles of behaviour only when dealing with the difficulties of managing 'problem behaviours'. Remember, though, that autism is diagnosed by a constellation of certain behaviours including social development, emotional development, communication, language, and thinking. It is the measurement of excesses or deficits in these behaviours that leads to the detection and diagnosis of autism. It is strange, then, that these behaviours are usually discussed without reference to the principles of behaviour.

Conclusion

Many of the parents in the PEAT group drifted into the group from other parent groupings because they were dissatisfied with the way in which these support groups operated. The main comment was that having a shoulder to cry on or being helped to 'cope with life with a disabled child' was necessary but it was not enough. Their initial reaction to Applied Behaviour Analysis usually contained some element of relief. At last somebody was going to show them how to deal with their child at home! Parents of the PEAT group have shown in this book what can be done when parents and professionals work in partnership to share a wide range of skills, both for the functioning of the group and for the enhancement of their children's potential. With appropriate guidance parents can function as therapists for their own children. They can be taught how to transform their knowledge of the principles of behaviour into procedures that are adapted to the needs of their child.

References

Chiesa, M. (1998) Are all therapies equally effective? *Invited address to The Experimental Analysis of Behaviour Group*. London, Easter conference.

Hawkins, R.P. (1972) *Psychology Today*, 11, 40.

Jordan, R., Jones, G. and Murray, D. (1998) *Educational Interventions for Children with Autism: A Literature Review of Recent and Current Research*. Final report to the DfEE, June.

Keenan, M. (1997) W-ing: Teaching exercises for radical behaviourists. In K. Dillenburger, M. O'Reilly and M. Keenan (eds) *Advances in Behaviour Analysis*. Dublin: University College Dublin Press.

Schopler, E. and Olley, J.G. (1982) Comprehensive educational services for autistic children: The TEACH model. In C.R. Reynolds and T.R. Gutkin (eds) *Handbook of School Psychology*. New York: Wiley.

Van Houten, R., Axelrod, S., Bailey, J.S., Favell, J., Foxx, R.M., Iwata, B.A. and Lovaas, O.I. (1987) *The Right to Effective Behavioral Treatment*. Kalamazoo: Report of the Association for Behavior Analysis (ABA) Taskforce on the right to effective treatment.

Walsh, P. (1997) Bye-bye behaviour modification. In K. Dillenburger, M. O'Reilly and M. Keenan (eds) *Advances in Behaviour Analysis*. Dublin: University College Dublin Press.

Colin's language
(four months after treatment was begun)

Colin's vocabulary now consisted of over 400 words and he was using verbs in short sentences, such as 'man climbing tree', 'here came Johnnie', 'man reading newspaper', 'teddy jumping on box'. He was able to take turns, complete nursery rhymes and songs, and sit with a book and point out the actions (he had started to pick out simple words, like 'go', 'man', 'stop' and could spell his name). He could follow simple directions such as 'go and put your coat on the chair', 'fetch me the lego from under the table', 'give Daddy the salt', 'get your shoes from the sitting room'. He could take turns at telling simple stories such as 'Three Billy Goats Gruff', 'Red Riding Hood', 'Goldilocks and the Three Bears', and 'Three Little Pigs'.

He also enjoyed 'reading' books on his own, such as Spot, Noddy, Tots TV, Postman Pat, Mr Men and the Ladybird series. He was able to pick up the older children's books and point out the things that interested him. From his speech therapy tasks he could select picture cards ('Give me teddy jumping on the box') and take turns saying 'Give me teddy jumping on table'. He knew the names of many of the children at Nursery and was able to point them out. He especially liked Robert (saying 'hold hands' on the way out) and would say 'Robert go home', and also seemed to like Norman (saying 'bye bye Norman').

At home Colin enjoyed mechanical/structural toys, building his lego into bridges, cars, lorries, helicopters, and stations. For example, he set up the playmobil home as a station and let the toy railway line run past the building. He used the dolls house for indoor activities, such as dolls getting up, going downstairs, getting 'brekslik' (breakfast).

By this time Colin also routinely asked for objects, Laura had been reinforcing his use of more complete sentences such as 'Give me some juice, please?', or 'Can I have some crisps, please, Mammy?' If Laura said 'what do you want', he answered by saying 'What you want? I'd like chocolate biksit please'. He said 'thanks', or 'thank you'. He also said 'no', or 'no thanks', if he didn't want something. If the item wasn't forthcoming immediately, he would say 'Do you hear me?' quite crossly.

Colin was now much more restrained. Having to stop and articulate his needs made him hold back and increased his compliance. He was still very fond of the story Three Billy Goats Gruff which he 'played' frequently, hiding under the table ('bridge') and jumping out (on his turned in toes, like the illustration in his book) singing 'I'm a troll fol de rol ... and I'm going to eat you for my supper'. He would play the part of the goats and end up 'go splash in the water'. He was now talking continually at play, not all of it is distinguishable, but much of it was clear, e.g., 'oh no', 'it's broken'; 'oh, quickly; get fire engine'; 'fix it; here came the engine'; 'beep, beep; there she went'.

Colin's vocabulary

In order to assess Colin's vocabulary, Laura put a list on the fridge door and took a note of each new word said by Colin. The list below shows the sequential order in which these words were acquired.

dog	apple	bat	sitting	bath	
cat	banana	trousers	stairs	bathroom	big bird
kangaroo	potato	pants	bed	sitting room	Impossible
giraffe	beans	T-shirt	steps	kitchen	Mr Sneeze
hippo	carrot	jersey	upstairs	bedroom	Teacher
monkey	coke	shirt	downstairs	bleach	William
spider	juice	fish	door	pen	answer
bee	milk	seaside	were	crayon	knows
tiger	tea	bicycle	open	drawing	brave
lion	coffee	telephone	flowers	painting	keys
horse	note	vacuum cleaner	trees	computer	silly
cow	cold	TV	grass	dish	butterfingers
sleep	sausages	mat	goats	own disk	fire engine
rabbit	chicken	bend	troll	Ghostbusters	shoes
guinea pig	meat	sketch	bridge	Indiana Jones	socks
bird	tomato sauce	music	over..	Scalextric	stove
car	eggs	rock	under..	Tuba ruba	cooking
lorry	chips	rock together	up	Tots TV	Cornflakes
truck	butter	clap (hands)	down	Tilly	music
coal lorry	seat	hands	all done	Tom	posting
brick lorry	table	feet	doctor	Tiny	Postman(Pat)
van	chair	toes	Mrs Tweed	Noddy	running
red	bread	eyebrows	station	Bigears	walking
blue	join	cheeks	Wendy	PC Plod	fingers
green	Corn Pops	more	bye bye	mouse	tractor
pink	Weetabix	mark	see you later	dolly	digger
purple	Cornflakes	ears	watch	Teddy	steam roller
yellow	Rice Krispies	clench(fist)	clock	Bert	motor bike
orange	weeks	eyes	I go	Ernie	light
square	bump	kiss	train	Elmo	turn on ...
rectangle	stop	head	tank engine	count	turn off ...
triangle	go	Crunchy nut	monster	cookie	put down
circle	coat	fall down	water	Gordon	toast
trailer	Patrick	crash	birthday	hankie	James
castle	Thomas	cracked	happy	crying	chance
alphabet	Daisy	dirty	sad	laughing	breakfast
excuse me	Domino	class	cross	may	dinner
please	Rover	flush	angry	boy	lunch
thank you	Pussy	toilet	sewing	girl	bus
thanks	picture	floor	sharp	hold hands	big
hen	book	helicopter	scissors	let go	broken
rooster	page	plane	brush floor	give me	building
goose	farm	chocolate	pat	back	bricks

Colin	the	Mars	elbows	corner	grey
me	and	Snickers	knees	round	No Martin
mine	to	Twix	digger	birthday card	No thank you
I	lone	penguin	clown	Santa Claus	Mickey
Ruth	each other	ginger snaps	pig	snowman	Karola
Suzanne	most of all	Smarties	school	snow	baby
Matthew	black	Milkyway	church	raining	here he is
Carol	brown	Milkyway stars	lolly	slippery	here she is
granny	soldier	crisps	ice-cream	hot	There's Mammy
Alan	policeman	hula hoops s	hopping	cold	there he is
Daddy	fireman	Maltesers	shops	cup	there she is
Mammy	ambulance	fighting	donkey	plate	garage
buttonhole	police car	bold	faster	dish	petrol
Norman	fire engine	standing	no	knife	water
Robert	garden	bedtime	yes	Madeline	piece
Sam	sky	Pedigree chum	deadly	spoon	monster
Sacha	moon	Whiskas	excellent	Yoghurt	Tele monster
Laura	Kit-e-kat	upside down	outside	goldfish	Tommy
Sarah	sun	Kit kat	sneeze	salt	help
Natasha	sunshine	Rocky	cough	sugar	what's that
Dean	stars	biscuit	piano	wet	help me
Christopher	walking	cookie	fiddle	reading	cushion
Johnstone	running	cake	Wowser	newspaper	harbour
sandwich	slippery	Captain Short	grass	shut up	house
sandwiches	crumbly (snow)	parsley	goodnight	fire	eat/eating
brush hair	give me my	Sage	darling	hug	same
sewing	may I have	doot-doot	round the	jammies	not the same
machine	some juice	(recorder)	corner	cuddle	teacher
jumped	dinner	chimney	coughing	football	come on
jumping	lunch	Where were you?	sneezing	snooker	be careful
very hungry	crisps	delicious	snoring	look at me	roll over
supper	don't	excellent	whisper	wash	poor teddy
be careful	bricks	need	now	brush teeth	give way
work	sticks	want	corner	milk	farmer
round	wolf (big, bad)	cottage	uphill	bridge	farmhouse
roundabout	soup	hop	downhill	straw	cuckoo clock
hammer	Sooty	long	watch out	Tin Tin	crunch
nail	Sweep	longer	screwdriver	Snowy	green grass
boat	Soo	shake	screw	Jess	train set
oars	Scampi	munch	butter		

Speech and language therapy

Jill Neeson

As a speech and language therapist my first contact with Colin was in December 1995, when he was aged three years ten months. At this stage he had already had some speech and language therapy (SLT) input at his local health centre.

During my initial visit to his home, Colin presented as a very active child. When shown a range of activities (toys, books, puzzles, miniature animals and people) he would approach the table and objects for a very brief moment and then move away. He showed no interest in initiating any interaction or in responding to communication both verbal and non-verbal, that was directed to him.

While displaying this 'approach and withdrawal' behaviour so often evident in children with autism, he did use a few single words to label the objects, but not to request them. He did not show understanding of single words. He was unable to select objects by name; he did not respond to his name or act on simple instructions such as 'sit down'. He made very little eye contact. He did briefly explore the objects but did not display any symbolic or imaginative play.

Based on the previous information and assessments available and on the observations made it was clear that Colin's communicative behaviour showed clear deficits in language development, social interaction and creativity/imaginative play.

The aims of speech and language therapy input at this stage were to:

- Improve eye contact
- Improve attention and focussing i.e. keeping 'on task'
- Improve anticipatory skills
- Improve auditory skills – listening/memory
- Improve turn-taking

Communication is a two way behaviour involving partnership between child and carer. It was extremely important to use short activities which would have intrinsic positive reinforcement and feedback for both parent and child. The 'Body Awareness Contact and Communication Programme' (Knill and Knill, 1992) provided a basis on which to build. This programme encourages the development of the above listed behaviours through music and movement programme.

This programme started in January 1996. Colin attended the local community clinic on a weekly basis for a 45–minute therapy session. This session started with an activity from the 'Body Awareness' programme which Colin found enjoyable and which helped him 'get set' for further language work.

Therapy session format

- 'Body Awareness' (Knill and Knill, 1992) programme (to 'get set' for further work).

- Further activities to improve auditory attention: e.g. sound/picture matching; copying sound sequencing.

- Specific language building tasks involving much role reversal and turn-taking to develop comprehension and expressive skills. Activities from the Derbyshire Language Scheme (D.L.S.) (Masidlover and Knowles, 1979) were included.

- Games and play activities to develop turn-taking and simple imaginative play.

Each task would be short. Often reinforcement was intrinsic at other times a favourite toy or puzzle would be offered for a short time on completion of a task.

During the first four months of therapy, together with input from other professionals and, most important, the daily reinforcement and generalisation of tasks provided by his mother at home, Colin made rapid progress.

Improvements noted were

- Eye contact.

- Auditory skills: attention and listening and auditory memory.

- Language comprehension: from single word comprehension to understanding of instructions with four information carrying words, (as described in Masidlover and Knowles, 1979).

- Expressive language: in picture description tasks Colin was now producing utterances of up to five words i.e. three connected ideas (Masidlover and Knowles, 1979), e.g. 'Teddy bears sit on the box'.

At this time, April 1996, Colin's parents persevered with their commitment to obtain a mainstream education for Colin. This was much against the current trend in Northern Ireland (Adams, 1993). Their perseverance paid off. Colin started mainstream school in September 1996.

Within school, speech and language therapy has continued. Colin is fortunate to have dedicated teachers and classroom assistants within a school which encourages inclusive education. His speech and language therapy programme is updated on a fortnightly basis in school. Repetition, reinforcement and generalisation work is carried out by his classroom assistant and teacher. There is regular liaison with his parents. His progress and ongoing communication needs are jointly re-evaluated on a regular basis.

Formal assessment has shown continued progress over the period April 1996 – February 1998.

Pre-School Language Scale – 3 (Zimmerman, Steiner and Pond, 1991)

Chronological Age	Equivalent Age	Standard Score	Percentile Rank
4 years 2 months	2 years 11 months	72	3%

Clinical Evaluation of Language Fundamentals – Pre-School (Wiig, Secors and Semel, 1992)

Chronological Age	Equivalent Age	Standard Score	Percentile Rank
4 years 11 months	3 years 7 months	80	9%
5 years 7 months	4 years 7 months	96	30%
6 years 0 months	6 years 5 months	103	58%

The tables above show Colin's chronological age at time of testing and his calculated percentile rank. The equivalent age reflects the median score obtained by children in each age group. Age equivalents compare a child's performance in relation to other children in the normative sample at that age. The standard score shows how far a child's score deviates from the average score. The above tests have standard scores, which have a mean of 100 and a standard deviation of 15. One standard deviation is often used as the criterion for describing a child as language disordered (i.e., a standard score of below 85 is seen as significant). The percentile rank indicates the percentage of children in the normative score who would obtain either the same score or lower on the test. At chronological age 4: 02 Colin scored a percentile rank of 3% which would equal or surpass only 3% of the children in that age group. At chronological age 6: 00 he showed a percentage rank of 58% which would equal or surpass 58% of children in that age group. This shows marked improvement over time.

The current speech and language therapy programme includes:

(1) Specific language tasks.

    (i) To improve Colin's understanding of abstract curriculum concepts.

    (ii) To improve planning and sequencing of expressive language for more narrative tasks e.g., relating events; retelling stories; giving descriptions and explanations.

(2) Social interaction skills building – self/other awareness; self monitoring of behaviours (Kelly, 1996)

(3) Joint management and problem solving of any communicative behaviour difficulties as they arise in school i.e., curriculum specific / social interaction difficulties.

As a speech and language therapist my first contact with Behaviour Analysis (BA) was in my college days (mid-1980s), when BA was not presented in a positive way. When I became aware that Colin's parents were using BA to help with his behaviour my immediate reaction was one of concern.

I feel that my initial reservations were based on the false premise that BA consisted of repeatedly 'drilling' the child in a clinical atmosphere far from the 'real' world and functional communication learning. However BA in its broadest sense is based on the premise that behaviour is repeated because it is reinforced, therefore if positive reinforcement is given to a desired behaviour, then behaviour can be shaped and changed. When I reviewed my own working practice as a speech and language therapist, my aims are for a child to achieve his/her optimum communicative potential, in other words, to develop and change the child's communicative behaviour. Therapy tends to be based on a series of tasks which include intrinsic or extrinsic rewards. Specific therapy targets are repeated, reinforced and generalised in functional settings. To parents already involved in BA this will already sound like a familiar approach. Also, the speech and language therapy programme and targets are based on detailed observation and formal assessment of the child's skill and needs (Van der Gaag, 1996). Each programme is individual and child specific. Skills are regularly reassessed and targets updated.

I believe it is imperative that a speech and language therapist is involved in assessing a child's communications skills, and in providing targets and suggestions for activities to achieve these targets and generalise them.

In summary, the BA approach has many advantages:

- The intensity of the input
- The empowerment of parents
- The positive approach to the child (as opposed to the 'can't/won't/don't attitude often found)
- The individualised and child specific approach
- The full range of targets, e.g., language skills; physical skills; self care skills
- The interdisciplinary approach
- The consistency.

References

Adams, F.J. (ed) (1993) *Special Education in the 1990s.* Harlow: Longman.

Kelly, A. (1996) *Talkabout.* Bicester, Oxon: Winslow Press.

Knill, M. and Knill, C. (1992) *Body Awareness Contact and Communication.* Cambridge: Living Development Aids. Living and Learning (Cambridge) Ltd.

Masidlover, M. and Knowles, W. (1979) *Derbyshire Language Scheme.* Derby: Derbyshire County Council.

Van der Gaag, A. (1996) *Communicating Quality 2.* London: The Royal College of Speech and Language Therapists.

Wiig, E., Secors, W. and Semel, E. (1992) *Clinical Evaluation of Language Fundamentals Pre-school.* London: The Psychological Corporation. Harcourt Brace Jovanich, Inc.

Zimmerman, I., Steiner, V. and Pond, R. (1991) *Pre-School Language Scale – 3.* London: The Psychological Corporation.

Colin's day

This was Saturday 29 June 1996. Colin was four years and four months old. This day was recorded approximately seven months into treatment. Part of the treatment at the time included the 'looking game'. Colin's usual routine so far included leaving for nursery at 8.45 a.m. and arriving home at approximately 12.00 noon but this is the first day of the holidays. Also it was extremely wet so he didn't get outside much.

7.30 am   He got up and went downstairs with Carol to watch TV. Laura went down after him and he showed her his red car and said 'Red car from Mrs Tweed' (Nursery school teacher).

7.40 am   Colin asked for breakfast. When asked 'What do you want?', he said 'cabbage' (laughed). Did the 'looking game' for 20 seconds. Chose toast, went to fridge for margarine, got jam from cupboard, talking in short sentences. Back in to watch early morning TV with Ruth and Carol who were eating breakfast too. Answered questions on programmes – 'What's he doing', 'What's that', etc. Talks out loud about interesting bits, turned to Laura to tell her 'train's in station'. Came around to say 'Felix is driving a train – that's silly'. Sat on Laura's knee and babbled on – bits of Red Riding Hood when a big hairy character appears and roars, smiles and laughs. Went to Ruth and sat beside her – she asked him things – 'What's happening?' Sat pushing Ruth gently with his feet and watching TV. Told Ruth, 'Here's teacher, there's school, time to go to school'. Got up and came over to climb over Laura. (Never sat absolutely still for long.) Did 'round and round the garden'. Laura asked 'Where's the red car'? Colin went to look for it in sitting room. Laura told him that she knew where it was – he asked 'Can I have my red car Mammy?' Went and got it from scullery (Laura opened door). Played on mat (not watching TV now). Chatting 'it's in the yard'. Went to bathroom. Laura followed him – he was drying his hands. Pretended he's just out of the bath when he saw Laura 'rub a towel'. Back to car on mat – 'car broken' and worked in engine compartment. Looked up at noisy bit on TV. Brought breakdown truck on to mat and was repairing red car. Laura left for work. Geoffrey (Colin's father) and Ruth continued to record.

8.15 am   Damp patches on both knees of trousers. Colin tried to clean. Transfixed by pirate cartoon.

8.19 am   Back to playing with car, rubbed knees.

8.21 am   Sat on Geoffrey's knee, watched TV.

8.29 am   Changed chairs, sat on chair and looked round.

8.37 am   Said 'Mickey fighting' and played fighting with Carol and Geoffrey.

8.40 am   Went to brush teeth.

8.42 am   Climbed behind Daddy at table – said 'bold'.

8.49 am   Sung Grand Old Duke of York, drove truck round Geoffrey's neck.

8.55 am	Still behind Geoffrey, singing.
9.05 am	Asks more breakfast 'because I'm hungry'.
9.30 am	Still singing and climbing behind Geoffrey – got dressed.
9.45 am	Matthew (finally) got up – Colin went to play with him.
9.47	Back to Geoffrey. Laura arrives back from work.
9.48 am	Sent to brush floor. Said 'Hello Mammy', playing with truck, 'put the sand'. Went and hugged Geoffrey. Got sweets (removed breakfast). shouting 'Ribbet' (rivit) as he made frog noises, jumped, swapped Ruth's green frog for his red one. Counting sweets – 'I got six – take away one – 5', 'Take away 2 – 4' etc. Ate sweets and watched Children's TV.
	Spat out small wine gum. Laura gave him a hanky – he said 'tidy up'. Adverts on. Went over to Ruth, watched coco pop advert, answers question 'it's a dinosaur'. Sitting on Ruth's knee – 'balloon broken' (TV). Gave Carol a sweet – gave one to Geoffrey – jumped up and down and said 'Give a Daddy'. Ran off into sitting room to eat sweets.
10.07 am	Leaning on Geoffrey watching TV. Came across to Laura, said 'Mickey fighting', grabbed hand, laughing.
10.10 am	Rocking Matthew in chair – Matthew had red car. He said 'Get red car', 'Can I have the red car Matthew because I play with it' – 'Yeah, I got it'. Played with red car and truck.
	Came out with Laura to collect milk and water plants. Tickled Pussy (cat) as she walked in shouting 'tickle, tickle', run around shouting 'Oh my plant, oh my plant'.
10.20 am	Dancing steps, tickled Pussy (who got out of her chair), jumped, jumped. Went into sitting room to play with cars, shouting and singing 'up jumped the scarecrow'. Back in kitchen, looked up at TV 'It's a Batman stuck', ran out saying 'Poor Batman'.
10.25 am	In wash house (Laura was putting on washing). He played with playmobil house and his red car and singing 'jingle, jangle scarecrow'.
10.32 am	Playing with Matthew – sharing car and watching TV.
10.37 am	Sat on Geoffrey's knee – showed left foot etc., repeating end of little Red Riding Hood.
10.48 am	Asked for drink of milk (in scullery). Got hold of Domestos bottle 'do you want to fight?' Left off to watch adverts.
10.50 am	Asked Matthew 'red car please, cause I want to play with it'. On Geoffrey's knee chatting 'Bump the railway line' with red car (reference to journey to nursery school).
11.00 am	Scary skeleton in story on TV – looked up. Said 'broken bicycle' as truck run over it on TV (boys on TV finds shiny yellow bicycle) – said 'yellow bicycle – red bicycle broken'. Sung Grand old Duke of York. Car pushed up on Geoffrey's shoulder 'when they're up, they're up' and pointed down 'when they're down, they're down'. Geoffrey got up. Sat in Geoffrey's chair, watching TV and playing with red car. Laura took red car away – asked for 20 'looking'. Gave him car – Suzanne took it and asked him where he got it 'present car' and 'Mrs Tweed gave red car'. Suzanne running it on floor – Colin got it and ran off with it.
11.10 am	Suzanne got red car back and crashed it again – he retrieved it and went into sitting room (Laura followed). He took off tyres and put them in the dumper truck. Laura told him to put them back and he shouted 'dumper

truck' and tipped out the tyres and put them back on the car. Lifted Telling Time book – at 11 o'clock he said 'it's time to go shopping and Mum she's tired. Time for outside'. We move the hands round 1 o'clock, 2 o'clock etc. ────── Played with book himself – 'supper time, story time' etc. Made a bridge with book – he and Ruth were putting truck through tunnel. Ruth and he were chatting. Ruth went to sort through books in kitchen, Colin stayed with his tunnel.

11.25 am Back in, into scullery while Laura answered front door. He dropped car in sink 'in the sea'. Others get crisps. 'Can I have a bag of Rollers, please Mammy because I'm thirsty', 'what?' because I'm hungry'. Counting to 20 'looking' – some false starts as Suzanne was racing his car – then he got crisps – had to guess which hand – 'is it in left hand?' Eating Rollers. Sitting in chair eating and watching Flintstones. Carol joins him on chair – he's pushing with his feet at chair arms, twiddling his toes etc. Others go into wash house to tidy up. Finished crisps, run across to Laura and touched her cheek – said 'sore cheek' and patted it. Helped himself to more crisps – had to put them back. Put empty packet in bin (under duress). Went and got a packet of chocolate biscuits – had to put them back. Laura closed the door and put him on chair – sitting

11.45 am fidgeting, watched Flintstones. Went into wash house, with others tidying up toys and cupboards. 'Get for Daddy'. Playing on computer. Left it to tidy up toys and took two pieces of road map floor puzzle.

12.10 pm Playing with floor puzzle and small cars – 'park in yard', 'crash', etc. Singing 'Old McDonald', playing, talking through car game.

12.30 pm Sitting on Geoffrey's back watching Grand Prix.

12.40 pm Back into wash house watching Suzanne adjust colours on Sega 'it's green – black'.

12.50 pm Playing with toys in kitchen. Said 'Daddy big colours – come see'. Took Geoffrey's hand and brought him out to see Sega. Came into sitting room to play with car.

1.00 pm Lunch – 20 'looking' then got his lunch at the table with the others.

1.05 pm Raced into sitting room to play. Returned to table to eat melon 'crunch' 'eat the crunch'. 'Zero bread' – 'zero, zero' counting empty plates. Danced on chair, made to sit down. Had more onion bread.

1.10 pm Finished, left and went upstairs – Laura followed – truck, police car and railway set out on bedroom floor, talking constantly 'stop, stop' and 'play with wee toys' etc.

1.25 pm Called to come down and go out – still laying track making bridges – on his own in bedroom but Ruth was directly across the hall doing homework on her bedroom floor.

1.30 pm Came downstairs, said 'Come on, upstairs, see train station, come on'. Told he had to get socks and shoes on and go out, he said 'No thank you, come see train, no go shops'.

1.40 pm Matthew and Colin in their room, Colin pushing Matthew in cupboard and telling story of Little Red Riding Hood (put Granny in cupboard). When Laura came in with shoes, played round and round the garden as she put them on. Came downstairs with Ruth, went into wash house and played on Sega (to 4th level) as we gathered up the others from outside etc. and got the dog in.

1.45 pm	Left to get into car. Talked in back of car 'Daddy, got lights, rattle rattle'. Children saw horse with blanket on and said it had a coat on, he said 'Got shoes on' (we'd seen a forge and horseshoes at Leslie Hill Open Farm on Thursday).
2.00 pm	Car park in town – Colin's 'wheels on bus' tape, singing with girls (Matthew protesting because he hates it).
2.05 pm	Got out of booster seat and tried to climb in front to do 'round and round the garden'. Sat back down for 'Grand old Duke of York' (Laura told him she would turn it off unless he sat down). Matthew took red car – got it back when his seat belt was on. Colin sung along with tape.
2.07 pm	Counting cars in car park – 'Going to Town' sung along with Runaway Train. Geoffrey came back, we go to Ann's house in next village. (Ann is Carol's friend). Her little sister came running out to 'see Colin' (she's 4). He smiles and said 'hello Ellen'. Sang and ate sweets on way home.
2.40 pm	Home – Colin didn't want to come in – 'No go in, play outside' but too stormy. Said 'hello Rover' to dog. Opened back door – blew in with storm and jammed lock – had to be brought into kitchen – got cross; smacked Laura. Told him off – smacked Laura again. Took car off him and made him apologise and hug. Returned car. He said 'draw car' as Laura was writing. Drew car.
3.00 pm	Eating piece of cake at table with others and watching TV (Sylvester and Tweety).
3.06 pm	Alan (neighbour's child) arrived. 'Hello Alan' – wanted to go out with Matthew and Alan (but they didn't want him) but agreed to do some work to get his special toys. Did 20 'looking' x 5 each
3.30 pm	Speech therapy cards and prepositions. Said 'go upstairs see Alan and Matthew' – ran out saying 'Matthew, Alan, play digger'. (They were in Matthew's room).
3.31 pm	Came down counting stairs. Took 'lift the flap' book (no digger – Alan wouldn't let him play with it). Decided he wanted toys (as promised). Went up to study 'get a garage, get truck, get rocket' 'watch out, there's a drill' (Geoffrey now drilling).
3.37 pm	Ruth and Colin played with four toys; Ruth pursuing him. Talking constantly – short sentences describing what he's doing. Showed me how to fix rocket to the trailer – 'down there' as he pushed pieces in. Came across to Ruth as she tried to fix the turtle castle.
3.45 pm	Alan and Matthew come downstairs. Alan wants to play with toys. Colin went to toilet but returned quickly. Played with Alan with garage – lots of instructions. Laura asked him where was Rocksteady and he said 'in the seat' and went to Ruth (she was with the castle) to show her. Went back to garage and handed Alan the breakdown truck to push up the ramp – Alan closed the turtle castle, and Colin opened it up for him when asked.
3.50 pm	Alan wanted to go out – Suzanne joined Colin on mat pushing and pulling things. Colin talked all the time – 'put away in the jail' (Rocksteady).
4.00 pm	Girls went outside (rabbit and Guinea pig to be fed). Colin left playing on mat.
4.03 pm	Went to toilet – washed his hands, dried them when told to. Returned to toys; then went and got dog. Back to toys – answered questions while he

played – e.g., 'What colour is Ellen's hair? (difficult, as it is red) etc. Girls came back in.

4.15 pm	Went into wash house – Ruth followed (Laura put toys away). Played on Sega.
4.20 pm	Still wash house – now reading Noddy book. Back to Sega – got an extra life in the game.
4.27 pm	Playing with Geoffrey's tools – 'buzzing' for cordless screwdriver. Laura went out of room – could hear him banging on scullery door as Geoffrey
4.30 pm	Went out with tools. When Laura came in Suzanne had turned on TV and they were watching adverts.
4.35 pm	Playing with cards. Run off to wash house; instructing Ruth while she played on Sega 'Get the money' 'kill the bird' 'watch the bubbles' 'get extra life' etc.
4.40 pm	Ran into kitchen. Robo cop is on TV – sat on rocking chair.
4.50 pm	Got up and went into sitting room – Ruth called him into wash house.
4.54 pm	All had cake at the kitchen table.
4.57 pm	Asked for a drink of milk – changed his mind to juice – counted to 30 'looking'.
5.00 pm	Went up (to the boys' room) to play with red car.
5.06 pm	Downstairs again – into wash house calling 'mess' to Geoffrey who was drilling.
5.07 pm	Playing with red car on mat in kitchen.
5.08 pm	Upstairs – counting. I asked him where he was going – 'upstairs' Why? – because', 'I want to play with toys', 'and Alan' 'and Matthew' (They have Colin's cassette player upstairs). Colin pretended to play the guitar.
5.15 pm	Still in bedroom, loading scrabble letters onto dumper truck (others sitting around listening to music).
5.19 pm	Called Alan and Matthew downstairs (Alan jumped off top bunk – he is very heavy and made a great bang). Ruth brought up some Noddy books and toys to Colin – he was building the floor puzzle.
5.25 pm	Alan went home – Colin said 'Goodbye Alan' and took over Matthew's Sega game – calling Geoffrey to come and see.
5.30 pm	Suzanne was playing Chase HQ and he was calling out her score.
5.36 pm	In kitchen – Geoffrey lying on mat reading, Colin was rolling on his back, chasing a melon round the floor. Laura took melon and he started to drive his red car round Geoffrey.
5.40 pm	Colin rolling on Geoffrey's back, half heatedly watching Dad's Army.
5.45 pm	Sitting on Geoffrey's shoulders (on floor) doing 'round and round the garden'.
5.46 pm	At kitchen table playing with fire engine. Laura went into scullery to make dinner.
6.03 pm	Laura followed him to bathroom – he had filled the sink and was washing cars and tractors. Came in and tipped up Pussy from chair (dog chased her).
6.05 pm	Played with Matthew on Sega.
6.07 pm	Read book.
6.09 pm	Played on Sega.
6.15 pm	Set the table 'fork to the left, knife to the right', salt and pepper, Went upstairs to bedroom.
6.27 pm	Brought down for dinner.

6.36 pm	Left table (not very hungry). Left room doing 'steps' then rushed back in 'come on Suzanne hold a hand, Suzanne, play computer because I want Suzanne'. Suzanne left table and set up change for him.
6.45 pm	Ran in saying 'dark – dark red'. Laura asked who was in the wash house and he said 'Ruth – on computer' (she was adjusting the colours strangely). Took some books into sitting room to 'read'.
6.50 pm	Sat on my knee and listened to new story (no timing) 'Rumpelstiltskin'
6.55 pm	enjoyed it and laughed a lot – lots of eye contact. Ran into wash house to join Ruth on computer.
7.00 pm	Came into scullery to ask for drink of coffee – counted to 30 'looking' (misheard and did 13 at first attempt). Finished coke, went out to sit on Geoffrey's back to watch Pets Win Prizes (Geoffrey pretending he wasn't watching it) – lying down and fidgeting. Got his feet under Geoffrey's jersey, pulled it over his own knees and said 'go to bed'. Feet out, bouncing on Geoffrey's back – sent off – Superman on TV. Went to look at Pussy in chair – said 'angry' had to said 'sorry' – he poked her and she
7.08 pm	scratched him. Went out to play on computer.
7.10 pm	Back in, climbing on Geoffrey's back shouting 'exercises'. Went upstairs – said 'going upstairs to the room'.
7.12 pm	Ruth followed him and they played with Stopcock.
7.13 pm	Came downstairs with red car. (Geoffrey took notes)
7.15 pm	'Bye car, go in the garage' – hides car.
7.16 pm	Retrieving car. Played.
7.20 pm	Opens Rover's mouth 'shark – teeth – shark'. Laura asked him 'Is Rover a shark?' 'No'. 'Is he a cat?' Wouldn't look up from staring at Superman on TV, so Laura turned his head and repeated it. He said 'No, Rover's a boy dog'.
7.25 pm	Something on TV jogs memory – 'Colin's sore finger – got blood'. Joking. 'Hi, Matthew' funny voices with Matthew.
7.27 pm	Playing 'fighting' game with Matthew in sitting room.
7.30 pm	Playing 'fighting' games in sitting room. Matthew went in to fiddle with Sega. Colin went with him and then made off with Suzanne's wool. Taken off him in sitting room.
7.37 pm	Sitting on Geoffrey's legs watching TV. Fidgeting.
7.43 pm	Standing on Geoffrey's back, watching TV.
7.50 pm	In wash house encouraging Sega players (Suzanne and self). Got into cupboard Geoffrey had just built up and bumped his head.
8.00 pm	Still advising on computer – 'get the money', 'get the frog' to Suzanne 'Go faster' etc.
8.10 pm	Got socks and shoes on to go and collect Carol from Ann's house. 'Right foot, left foot' etc.
8.15 pm	Answering questions on Rumpelstiltskin 'what's my name?' Got Geoffrey's hand and said 'let's go car'. Singing in car to nursery rhyme tape. Got out of car at Ann's and ran about holding Ellen's hand. Held hamster – liked silver one. Cried when Ann put golden hamster on his knee in car. Singing on way home.
9.00 pm	Home. Didn't want to come in – rode on bicycle but *very* cold and stormy. Put on pyjamas when we got in – resisted Geoffrey so Laura put them on. Asked for supper. Counted to 30 'looking' (3 false starts). Chose supper –

Carol refused Breakaways so he went back and chose Rockys. Asked him about his car journey. Told us where he had been. Brushed his teeth (Ruth). gathered up red car and fire engine.

9.10 pm   Kissed us goodnight and went upstairs. Got into bed, with car and fire engine. Others wandered in and out, reading to him (Ruth again) but he didn't get out of bed. Fell asleep.

9.30 pm   I left for work. No further movements.

Subject Index

Author Index